Divination with Diloggún

A Beginner's Guide to Diloggún and Obi

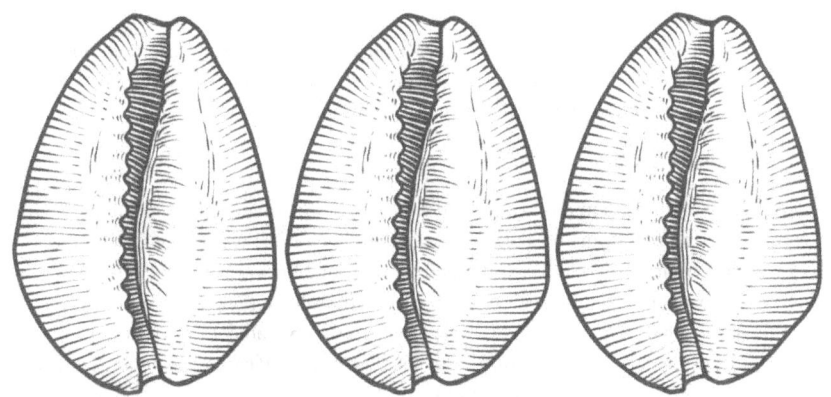

MONIQUE JOINER SIEDLAK

Oshun
Publications

Divination with Diloggún: A Beginner's Guide to Diloggún and Obi
© Copyright 2021 by Monique Joiner Siedlak

ISBN: 978-1-950378-89-0

All rights reserved

The content contained within this book may not be reproduced, duplicated or transmitted without direct written permission from the author or the publisher.

Under no circumstances will any blame or legal responsibility be held against the publisher, or author, for any damages, reparation, or monetary loss due to the information contained within this book, either directly or indirectly.

Legal Notice

This book is copyright protected. It is only for personal use. You cannot amend, distribute, sell, use, quote or paraphrase any part, or the content within this book, without the consent of the author or publisher.

Disclaimer Notice

Please note the information contained within this document is for educational and entertainment purposes only. All effort has been executed to present accurate, up to date, reliable, complete information. No warranties of any kind are declared or implied. Readers acknowledge that the author is not engaged in the rendering of legal, financial, medical or professional advice. The content within this book has been derived from various sources. Please consult a licensed professional before attempting any techniques outlined in this book.

By reading this document, the reader agrees that under no circumstances is the author responsible for any losses, direct or indirect, that are incurred as a result of the use of the information contained within this document, including, but not limited to, errors, omissions, or inaccuracies.

Cover Design by MJS

Cover Image by lisovskaya and lotas @depositphotos.com

Published by Oshun Publications

www.oshunpublications.com

Other Books in the Series

Divination Magic for Beginners
Divination with Runes

Contents

Introduction	xi
1. The Journey from Africa	1
2. The African Diaspora Religions	5
3. Cosmology & Creation	15
4. The Saints, Spirits, and Orishas	21
5. What is Divination?	47
6. Obi Divination	53
7. Diloggun Divination	61
8. Recipes	87
9. The Medicine of the Yoruba	95
10. The Importance of Prayer	99
11. The Concept of Death	103
Conclusion	109
References	113
About the Author	121
More Books by Monique	123
Last Chance	127
Thank You!	129

Introduction

From the very beginning, Africa has shown immense growth and almost unmatched strength in the diversity and richness of the empires and traditions that make up her soul. She has raised great kings and queens who fought off everything around them to protect their people. Africa has birthed the Great Benin Walls, the greatest earthwork in the history of the world, rumored to have once been longer than the Great Wall of China and used 100 times more building materials than the Egyptian pyramid of Cheops (Koutonin, 2020). She has observed countless more births and deaths than any other landmass because she is the origin of humanity. She is the center of the world (Beres, 2019).

Her essence holds music, poetry, and dance, waves of ecstasy, and her people, as diverse and scattered across the world as they are, remember the sound of her calling them. In their blood courses, the sound, and rhythm of their home. They may not be conscious of why they sing and dance in another tongue or why the drumbeat belongs to their tears, but she remains inside their hearts.

It took three to four centuries for what is known as The

Atlantic Slave Trade to transport approximately ten to fifteen million enslaved Africans away from their home and into the Americas. The journey alone killed many. Over the period between their capture and employment across the Atlantic sea to the Americas, thirty to forty percent of them died. We do not realize that the Catholic church in the 15th century gave Portugal the right to trade and plunder as they saw fit. To ultimately "reduce their persons to perpetual slavery" (Elliott & Hughes, 2019).

Divination with Diloggún has been written to add to the many voices that are now waking up to the old spirits and writing down what they know from this rich and growing culture. This book is not simply a guide to your divination practice but a gift to the Orishas to celebrate the strength of spirit that remains even after the pain and bloodshed. It holds within its words great love for the diversity in the spirit, which was born with the first breath of Nana Buluku inside the void of original thought. It holds within its sentences a blessing that you will find your connection with the very spirit of life inside the divine essence of the African soul.

Whether you are of African or European descent, understand that the cruelty which ensued does not run in our veins, only the spirit of devotion. The digital age holds great potential for spiritual unity across the seas instead of a divide like it has been for many centuries. Spirit is spirit, and each spiritual essence contains a particular design akin to our own experiences. The old church may have been the ruler of man, but spirit has always remained, and regardless of the power that man thinks they have, we are born of spirit, and it will always be our parent.

The ancestors still walk alongside those who choose to remember them. While we live our busy days in faster-growing economies and seemingly more significant empires of technology, the power of the old rulers still breathes in the

Introduction

practices. The power and wisdom still live in the dances of the Orishas and the answers found in the cowries.

Within Divination with Diloggún, there are prayers under each of the Orishas to make contact. Prayers to the Saints who are interchangeable with the spirit of each Orisha. It really depends on how you choose to connect with the spirit of the deities. It is often thought that Orishas are Gods and Goddesses, which they are not. The various offshoots of the Yoruba traditions do not follow a hierarchy, as is seen in many monotheistic and polytheistic religions. Each entity has a place and governs a natural phenomenon or a human one. Therefore they all have an importance that is not managed the same way as mainstream ideologies are. Please note that the prayers are not taken from any of the religions. Nor do they hold any attribution to a specific branch. They are my own work in dedication to the core of the spiritual essence of the Yoruba beliefs. Use them as you wish within your divination practices or even within the time dedicated to devotion.

The divination aspect of the Obi and Diloggún methods described herein are included to be empowered in your understanding. The methods and uses behind the simplicity and accuracy in Obi and the mathematical precision in the Diloggún take many years to learn and master. While Obi divination is a divination practice that can be used immediately to attain results, the Diloggún requires a great many years. In many circles, it is said that only an initiated priest or priestess may divine with the Odu Ifa.

Regardless of your choices, the tools are in your hands. Respect is not a choice but a prerequisite within any work pertaining to spiritual work as well as faith. There is an excellent preconception that the African spirits and ways of life have almost primitive energy within the human mind. Through my own experience, I have found the spiritual wisdom in divination practices and ancient lore indispensable

Introduction

to my own life. All the information contained within this book is as relevant as it was back then. I wish that you may find great happiness within these pages. May your answers be truthful and always in line with the great spiritual network of all that is within the beauty of the African soul.

ONE

The Journey from Africa

AFRICA GAVE BIRTH TO THE WEALTHIEST MAN IN THE HISTORY of the world, who was the ruler of the Mali Empire, founded in 1235 AD, Mansa Musa. His empire forged the constitution known as *The Division of the World* (HomeTeam History, 2018). He was the wealthiest man in history and a ruler of one of the first Islamic empires in Africa. Islam as a religion became a standard business etiquette between the rulers and the traders. It was to forge a better relationship between areas of interest. Therefore the Islamic faith became common among the elite. The other religious practices and cultural customs remained with the common people. Many of these ordinary people were taken as slaves during the trans-Atlantic slave trade (Mr. Z, 2018).

Before we look through the eyes of eleven-year-old Akintoye - a fictitious tale based on actual events to describe what the people went through when reaching the new world - we must first understand that Africa is more extensive than any map really shows us (Fischetti, 2015). Within this distortion of the continent's size, as well as the picture that has been painted of Africa having no history and being a poverty-stricken continent since the first human walked on her soil, we have been steered wrong (African Elements, 2020). Africa is one of the most diverse collections of religious views, spoken and written dialects, and people worldwide. There are an estimated 2000 languages spoken by approximately 3000 different ethnic groups (Allen, 1970).

The statistics above just touch the tip of the iceberg when we compare it to any other continent. Africa is an entire world by herself. In this incredibly rich and resourceful world, the strength of the Yoruba and other nations' spirituality was born. It was in the capture of the African people where these views were transformed across ocean and land, through masters and war, through adaptation, eventually, into what we have in front of our eyes today. When we understand this, we also understand that even though we would like to believe that a particular way of life is practiced like it was back then, it is not. This would be impossible because the world back then was vastly different, as were the people's thinking. The very air they breathed is not the air we breathe today (Black, 2010). Spirituality is in both the heart and mind of the devotee. It is within the core of the specifics of each teaching that we see the religious similarities. There are thousands of different ways to connect to spiritual energy. The splitting of the various Yoruba-born religions was inevitable to suit the diversity in the devotional needs of the people.

A Tale Through the Eyes of Little Akintoye

It's cold. My skin is itching from the whiplashing of the seawater that pours through the wooden boards above my head. I keep trying to scratch, but my hands are tied to the man next to me, and he won't move for me. Maybe he will, but our fathers are not from the same village, so I do not even know how to ask him. He is different from me. The scars on his face said he has been through more than I had. I'm hungry, and I do not think I will ever see my brothers again. I do not know how long we have been on this boat. It is my first time, and I do not like it. I do not know if those men will come back down again to give us water. I wish Yemaya could turn the sea into freshwater, just for one sip... just one.

    I was sleeping. It must have been about ten moons ago. My mother and father had gone out to the fields. I was not feeling well, and my brothers had gone off to play. I do not know what happened; I went to sleep and woke up in a strange place. They were screaming at me in a tongue I did not recognize and hitting me with a piece of wood. I got to my feet, and I knew what had happened then. I had been taken as a slave and kidnapped for another family. How far I was from home could have been anyone's guess. Mother and father had always warned us of this. We knew that we would be the last time we ever saw our family if we were kidnapped. Olodumare! I wept. I wept until I remembered how my father taught me to be strong. I was to follow in his footsteps. I was to run the village with my brothers. We would be deciding everything for our people. This was not my fate.

    Olodumare knew my fate. I would be strong. I tended the fires of six families before being chained to this unstable wooden ship that I had only heard tales of. Not even my parents knew of these pale-faced men who screamed and drank and hit everything around them. They were like the dogs at home that could not be tamed. They beat me before tying me to this man next to me. There were many of us dragged into this ship. Some of us screamed. Some fought so bravely they did not make it onto the ship. Their bodies were thrown over the side into the sea to sleep with Olokun. Their language was firm. Their hair was like the Northern people's. They exchanged beer and cloth for my body many times. I missed my mother's hands in the darkness when no one was looking. I wept for the laughter of my father when he was playing Ayo, and he won. I missed the tree behind our home. I missed the smell of my home—the smell of safety. I learned before this ship that I would never go home. I know my mother always said Olodumare would guide me and watch me.

    I sit here now. I am scared, itchy, cold, hungry, and alone. I have the stories of my Olodumare in my heart. I will always remember the words of my mother. I will keep my God close, and I will never let him go. I will never let her go.

TWO

The African Diaspora Religions

"I INQUIRED OF THESE WHAT WAS TO BE DONE WITH US; THEY gave me to understand we were to be carried to these white people's country to work for them. I then was a little revived, and thought, if it were no worse than working, my situation was not so desperate: but still I feared I should be put to death, the white people looked and acted, as I thought, in so savage a manner; for I had never seen among any people such instances of brutal cruelty; and this not only shown towards us blacks but also to some of the whites themselves" (Equiano, 2015).

THE ABOVE EXCERPT is taken from the life account of Olaudah Equiano, who came from the Kingdom of Benin, now known as Southern Nigeria. His book is one of the most historically correct accounts of the lives that slaves during the Trans-Atlantic Slave Trade had to endure. He was taken from his home at age 11.

The slaves who walked on the rich African soil were once ripped from their homes, stolen from everything they held dear. Even when they were beaten and killed while crossing the vast ocean, they saw Yemaya in the waves. They never forgot that Olokun knew the secrets of the future as the Orisha lay in the depths of the sea, waiting.

Now there are more than 100 million active practitioners within any one of the African diasporic religions. That number is growing by the day. There is no devil, no evil, no master of black arts in these ways of life. Instead of perceiving life as black and white, good and evil, the African diasporic religions have a universal map of how life is in reality. Each aspect of our life is covered within the practices; each element also has a solution when needed. Through the deep, intricate connections with the Orishas, Loa, or through ritual, each of the branches of the Yoruba religion provides a pathway to peace and fulfillment of life's purpose.

There is much hatred for what ensued throughout the old world. The respect that needs to be awarded to any religion or spiritual path that managed to survive should be more tremendous than ever to ensure that their suffering was not for nothing. However, we should not find hatred in our hearts for something which is dead and gone. Instead, we should build the blessings and strength of spiritual endurance in our souls. We should reach into the spiritual truths and grab hold of the essence that persisted in the hearts of men and women, regardless of their trials. We should see the beauty of spirit that carried them across the sea and into this very day.

Of course, each of the mouths that spoke their version of the religions crossed the seas, experienced suffering, and were torn from everything they knew and held dear. The digital age has allowed for the Yoruba religions of today to have some influence from the devotees that are left in Africa. Many places, such as Nigeria, with a population approximated at 203.5 million, have only two percent practicing the old religions or no religion (Nigeria, 2020). There is much fighting between the radical groups in the United States and in Africa. Confrontational monotheistic groups do not understand that the African religious diaspora is also monotheistic. Their difference lies in their respect for the world around them. Such brutality shown among people about faiths cannot be proven or disproven, except in the practitioner's heart. All life should be celebrated and venerated. Spirit permeates every part of our existence. To be given the chance of freedom to devote our lives to its miraculous divinity is the prayer for every devotee of every religion.

The Yoruba Religions

Not only did the Yoruba people survive, but their religion survived. Their faith survived inside the beliefs that were forced upon them. Both Catholicism and Protestantism were forced upon the people. They accepted it, adopting the new spiritual entities as their own, literally. This is known as a syncretic religious practice (Masquelier et al., 1997). Interestingly, the older religions which revere all forms of life are falling out of popularity with the people in Africa. Today, it is estimated that 40% of African worship happens through strict Christianity in the South, and another 40% attributed to Islamic worship in the North of Africa (Chiorazzi, 2015).

Let's leave out the primordial aspects of the cosmology of the Yoruba. We see a very monotheistic idea of religion with Olorun as the chief God of the Sky. Olorun is also known by other names such as Olodumare and Olofin-Orun (Idowu, 1995). To understand the nature of Olodumare and the primordial beginning of the universe, one would have to throw out all Western thinking and understand that Olodumare is the first beginning. Like a puzzle that is separated, we find the pieces which make up the divine Orishas. These Orishas together make up Olodumare. Beyond this, it must be understood that Yoruba, at its core, had four fundamental principles of living. These principles are found alongside other incredible life lessons within the *Sacred Oracles of Ifa* (Vanzant, 2020), which are considered the sacred scriptures of the

Yoruba people. The four principles, according to Yoruba High Priestess Iyanla Vanzant, are:

- The first principle speaks about your belief in the supreme creator of your choice. Complete and utter devotion is required. This faith must not be questioned or denied. In Yoruba tongue, the word for this ultimate creator is Olodumare.
- The second principle speaks about the importance of the ancestors. This principle advises you to have a respectful and lasting relationship with those who came before you, the culture, and the clan. High Priestess Vanzant states that what Western spirituality calls angels, the Yoruba call ancestors.
- The third principle speaks about the relationship that you have with your parents and family here on earth. It says that you are blessed by keeping this relationship strong and looking after your parents and family.
- The fourth principle speaks about the importance of your relationship with your community. Like the ones before, this relationship should always be kept in order and stay as positive as possible.

These tenets mentioned above belong across the board within all Yoruba-born spiritual paths. However, it is not enough to have a neat origin of every religious and spiritual path born out of the original Yoruba way. To explain it in this linear fashion would rob the below-mentioned spiritual paths of their own cultural richness from other parts of Africa. The exact trace and similarity sit within the Yoruba people and their culture. Still, there is so much more diversity that we have to understand. Although they all originated from the same motherland and have their similarities, they are nothing like each other (Kerestetzi, 2018).

Haitian Vodou

Haitian Vodou was born out of the 17th and 18th Centuries and other forms of Yoruba-influenced spiritual paths. Haitian Vodou was, however, only made an official religion in Haiti in 2003 (Carol J. Williams, Tribune Newspapers: Los Angeles Times, 2018). One of the slaves, who was more influential in its birth than any other, was François Makandal. François Makandal lost his arm while operating a sugar cane mill. He was no longer useful in the field or in the mills and sought another route for livelihood. In this quest, he ran from the plantation and went to form a maroon community. Maroon communities were established all across America and consisted of large groups of African slaves who escaped the plantations where they worked (*Slavery and Remembrance*, n.d.).

With his involvement in the Macaroon communities, he began to broadcast his knowledge of plants and their healing properties to the other slaves and people. He became very well known for his healing abilities, but soon after this started taking off, he came up with a plan that could mean the people's freedom. He would supply the slaves with poisons instead of healing herbs to give to their masters (The Choices Program, 2017). The masters began to die, and no one knew the reason behind this; they even called Makandal to see if he could be of assistance. He was later known as The Lord of Poison, and it is said that he was responsible for the death of more than 6000 people (Simpkins, 2016).

His uprising and rebellion are among the most pivotal points of the birth of Haitian Vodou. The peculiarities around his death further magnified his claims on supernatural powers. He was burned at the stake but escaped the first attempt. Unfortunately, when he was bound the second time, he did not escape (*Slavery and Remembrance*, n.d.).

In the tale of the night that changed everything, it is said that in the darkness of the woods of Bois Caiman in August

1971, the slaves gathered in ritual. One of the women present was possessed by Ezili Dantor, also known as the Black Madonna. She slit the throat of a Creole pig, and all who were present drank its blood and vowed to kill the white settlers and gain their freedom (Wall & Clerici, 2015). The tale continues to speak of how the "world's richest colony was overthrown, and the first black republic proclaimed." Ira Lowenthal, a Vodou art collector, and anthropologist from New Jersey, states that Vodou is the best thing that ever happened to racism. He also speaks extensively on the pride of the Vodou practitioners. This dignity is found in the non-judgemental freedom of the heart of Haitian Vodou (Wall & Clerici, 2015).

To explain the religious structure of Haitian Vodou, Lynne Warberg says that the practitioners are "70 percent Catholic, 30 percent Protestant, and 100 percent voodoo" (2021). Haitian Vodou does not express itself through Orishas. Instead, they have a wide range of intermediary spirits called Iwa, who work between the almighty Bondye and themselves. Many Catholic saints have also been attributed to the various Iwa. There are two types, the Petwa Iwa, evil spirits, and the Rada Iwa, who are benevolent (Dialogue Institute, 2020).

Candomblé

Candomblé originated through the slaves that landed in Brazil during the 19th century. Candomblé has profound influences from Yoruba, Islam, and Roman Catholicism. Candomblé's main objective is to live in harmony with nature through worship and devotion to the Orishas (Herbstein, n.d.). Candomblé, like Umbanda, has many similarities, except the aspect of ritual sacrifice (Animal Sacrifice In Brazilian Folk Religion, n.d.). The sacrifice of animals is used to please the Orishas and maintain a good relationship between divinity and humanity.

Candomblé believes that every practitioner has their own Orisha, who is part of them and their path since birth. This Orisha connection is almost like a guardian angel and protects the practitioner throughout their lives. The world view within Candomblé is neither evil nor good. In fact, your destiny is something that must be fulfilled, regardless of the nature of the human perception surrounding it. There is just destiny, and nothing is portrayed in the typical black and white aspects. The God who rules over all Orishas is Olodumare. Olodumare communicates through Exu, who is a messenger deity, and through the Orishas. There used to be over 200 Orishas; now, there are only 16 main ones, venerated at once within an Orisha ceremony. This was to provide space for devotion to the diverse people from Africa. Back home in Africa, an entire group of people would worship one Orisha. Now all 16 main ones are incorporated to give importance to all.

Axé is the living force of the practitioners of Candomblé. No practitioner is ever cremated because this would destroy their axé; instead, they are buried to allow the axé to be given back to the earth and her people (Landes & Cole, 2006). Candomblé practitioners are said not to pray conventionally but to sing to their Orishas in the way they would in ritual (SELKA, 2010).

Umbanda

Umbanda is a hybrid religion mixing elements of Candomblé, Kardecist Spiritism, Catholicism, and other indigenous African factors. Umbanda may be born out of these religious elements. Still, even before its prominence in the twentieth century, Umbanda is a strictly Brazilian religion almost exclusive from any other African religion (Engler, 2012).

There are a wide array of variations within Umbanda. Therefore, it is almost impossible to outline the precise belief structure within Umbanda's core. There are a few similarities, though, and these are summarized below (Engler, 2012):

- Umbanda places great emphasis on spirit-possession
- Possessions are not from deity but rather from disembodied spirits such as:
- Caboclos - well-intentioned healing spirits
- Pretos Velhos - former slaves that are humble and Christianized
- Exus - dangerous spirits usually belonging to crossroads, who are wise and able to undo the work of other exus.
- Pombas Giras - these are the female counterparts of the exus, who have a sexual orientation
- Boiadeiros - hybrid white spirits seen as cowboys
- Ceganos - gypsies
- The Orishas are seen to have never lived human lives
- Orishas govern the seven lines where the spirits of the light fall under
- Umbanda is a religion that allows all races, creeds, and walks of life to experience the divine - there is no prejudice
- Practitioners are referred to as Umbandistas

Santeria

Known as *The Way of the Saints*, Santeria has its roots in Cuba but is practiced today across Latin America, Europe, and the Caribbean. Like other Yoruba-influenced religions, Santeria believes in one singular godhead. In Santeria, God is referred to as Olodumare. The Orishas are worshipped in the same understanding as aspects of the all-powerful deity. Even though Santeria shares much with the other religions, there are minute differences within its core, known only to its practitioners. Divination is of great importance to Santeria worshippers. From this, much of the divination in this book comes from (de Armas, n.d.).

Trinidad Orisha

Trinidad Orisha is a mixture between spiritual baptism and Orisha worship. Devotees have adopted the term Shango Baptist because Trinidad Orisha is also known as Shango. There are, however, reported to be elements of Islam, Hinduism, Sufism, Judaism, Kabbalah in the belief system of the Trinidad Orisha way of life. Like with all Yoruba-born religions, drumming, singing, and praying are very important.

THREE

Cosmology & Creation

THE YORUBA COSMOLOGY AND TALE OF HOW THE WORLD OF humanity came to be is a rich and awe-inspiring one, sharing much detail with that of some Hindu philosophies. Before we describe the beginning of the world and how Olodumare created and continues to create each human being, let us look at how the Yoruba views the cosmos.

Think of the cosmos as a closed sphere. Above is what Western minds would call heaven. The Yoruba call this Orun or igba aiye; it is also translated as the otherworld, similar to the Celtic understanding of the word, which is different from an underworld. The lower part of the sphere of the cosmos is known simply as aiye, which is translated to mean the material world. It is said that when we merge the understanding of the material and the otherworld that we begin to understand the intricate secrets hidden from normal view.

Those who fall closer to the material world are known as the Ologberi or *the Unknowing Ones*. These are the uninitiated ones and children. Above them, now arriving closer to the igba aiye, are the *Knowing Ones*, who are the Alawo and the Alase. These are the herbalists, initiated practitioners, kings, queens, priests, and diviners. The Spirits, ancestors, and

Orishas are found between the top of igba aiye and the material world of *Knowing Ones*. Between the *Knowing Ones* and the Orishas, spirits and ancestors are the intermediaries - Elegba, Ifa (Orunmila), and Esu (Harvey, 2015).

Creation of Humanity

Once upon a time, before the first human, Oludumare, thought about creating solid earth. This idea, once thought about, was put into action immediately. Olodumare called the Orisha of arch divinity, Obatala. Olodumare gave Obatala a leaf of loose earth, a pigeon, and a five-toed hen.

Obatala was given the duty of creating a solid earth with these three tools. He went immediately to a spot on the liquid waste that he thought was perfect and threw down the leaf of loose soil. He set the five-toed hen and the pigeon loose, and they began scattering the earth all over. Once they had covered enough of the watery waste, Obatala returned to Olodumare to proclaim that the job had been successfully completed.

Olodumare sent a chameleon down to see that it was indeed satisfactory. Olodumare chose the chameleon for his disciplined mannerisms and his ability to assess any situation with great speed. The chameleon made two trips. On the first trip, he returned and said that while the job had been successfully completed, the area was too wet to be used. On his second trip, he proclaimed the area fit for use.

Obatala was satisfied and sent Obatala back down to make the earth beautiful. This time Obatala was joined with Orunla. Four trees were given to plant on the earth. Oreluere was the name of the being who would lead the dwellers of earth from heaven to earth. These first beings became the beginning of humanity. Both Obatala and Orunla prayed then for rain from Olodumare, and rain began to fall. Obatala was left with another job that he continues to this day. That is to fashion each and every human being. Obatala sculpts each human being from the sacred earth. It is Olodumare, though, who gives them the breath (emi) of life. Obatala creates as he wishes, each human being, different from the next one. It is on a special day that he sculpts those humans who have a visible uniqueness to them.

In another creation story, Olodumare is surrounded by many Orishas, both male and female. Olodumare is still seen as beyond gender and encompasses neither masculine nor feminine identity. Olodumare and the Orishas made their home a young baobab tree. Even though Olodumare told the Orishas that they could travel across the entire sky and roam as they pleased, they were all too happy to remain in the young baobab tree where their life was uncomplicated and perfect.

All the Orisha were satisfied except one Orisha, Obatala. Obatala went to the edge of the young baobab tree and peered over the edge. Through the mist, he saw that there was only a watery abyss as far as the eyes could see. He decided that he wanted to create something. As the sculptor and designer of the cosmos, he went to Olodumare and asked him to allow him to go to the watery abyss and create land so that there could be beings on it. Olodumare was extremely pleased to hear that at least one of the Orishas wanted to actually leave the young baobab tree and do something besides lounge around all the time. He agreed, and Obotala immediately went to Orunmila, the Orisha who could see into the furthest reaches of time. Obatala asked Orunmila to help him see what would be needed for his mission to be successful. Orunmila immediately fetched a tray with crushed baobab powder on it. He threw 16 palm kernels onto the tray and studied the markings that they made. He repeated this eight times.

Eventually, after much contemplation, Orunmila spoke up and told Obatala to get a chain of gold, maize, palm nuts, and sand together. He added that Obatala had to carry all the

Orishas' personalities with him, which were contained in the sacred egg. Obatala then went to retrieve gold from all the Orishas to make the gold chain. Once he had enough gold, he went to the goldsmith who melted the gold and created a chain. Obatala realized he had forgotten the hook and asked the goldsmith to shorten the chain and add a golden hook to the end of it. While the hook was being prepared, Obatala gathered all the sand across the sky and placed it inside a snail shell. He added crushed Baobab powder to the snail shell. He packed it along with maize, other unmentioned seeds found around the home of the Orishas and wrapped the egg containing all the personalities of the Orisha into his jacket. He kept the egg close to his chest so that it would not be subjected to freezing temperatures during the journey.

Obatala was ready for the journey. He took the chain and hooked the end into the sky. He began his descent and journeyed down the golden chain for seven days. Eventually, at the end of the seventh day, he reached the bottom of the chain. He hung there, unsure of what his next move would be, staring into the watery abyss until he heard the voice of Orunmila shouting to him to use the sand.

Obatala carefully reached into his bag and retrieved the snail shell which held the sand and the Baobab powder. He threw this mixture into the watery abyss. At once, the sand hit the watery abyss as if it were ground, and it spread quickly far and wide, as far as the eye could see. The sand solidified, and the first image of the earth was born. Obatala looked in amazement and still did not know what to do. He hung on the end of the chain until he could take it no longer, and his heartbeat so hard in his chest that the sacred egg burst open and the Sankofa bird who holds within it the spirit of all Orishas escaped. Like a storm, the bird flew across the sand. With the power of all the Orishas' personalities, it created the lowlands, the highlands, and the dunes.

Eventually, after watching all of this, Obatala let go of the chain. Where he landed, he called that place Ife or the land which divides the waters. He did not give another moment to standing around and began exploring the newly created land. As he walked, he dropped the seeds that he had collected around the young Baobab tree. As they hit the land, they grew into large trees and plants. As Obatala walked, the world became green and luscious behind him.

After walking and exploring for what seemed like ages, Obatala stopped at a small pond and bent down to take a drink of water. As he did this, he saw his reflection and was pleased. He sat down next to the pond and took a piece of the dark clay earth into his hands, and molded it into the shape he had seen in his reflection. When he had finished one, he began another, carefully molding the features as he saw them within the water. Eventually, Obatala had created many bodies from the dark soil of the earth.

After all this work, Obatala was so thirsty that he grabbed the juice from the palm trees and fermented it. He drank and drank to quench his thirst but eventually, he became too intoxicated to worry about thirst anymore. Obatala returned to complete his work of molding the dark clay. This time he was not methodical, and he created from his artistic intellect. He made many without eyes, some with more limbs than needed, others without any limbs at all. After a while, he had many of these beautiful creations, and he marveled at his work.

Olodumare heard the commotion from the land and wanted to know what was happening with Obatala. He sent a chameleon down to the earth, and the chameleon returned after discussing matters with Obatala. The chameleon told Olodumare that Obatala was saddened that he created all these magnificent forms, but none had life. Olodumare heard Obatalas plea and gathered the gasses from the space beyond the sky. He then sparked these gasses into an enormous explosion which he quickly shaped into a giant fireball. He sent this fireball to Ife. The fireball dried all the lands that were still wet and baked all the clay figures fashioned by Obatala.

Olodumare then blew his breath down and across all of Ife. Each and every figurine came to life, and these people were the first people of Ife (*Creation Stories*, n.d.).

FOUR

The Saints, Spirits, and Orishas

Within the Yoruba-born religions and ways of life, we find an entire array of different spiritual energies. The spirits all have different names, and some were once human, whereas others were not. The Orishas were created by Olodumare himself for the purpose of protecting creation.

To understand the design of the Orishas, we need to look at something called the Diamond Theory. If you look at a diamond, it has many facets or faces. Each of these is different; we can equate them to the various Orishas, and even the Loa and various spiritual energies. The faces may be different, but they all still belong to the diamond, which in this case would be Olodumare (Herren, n.d.).

The number of Orisha and spirits vary according to the belief system. In some instances, there may be said to be 400 plus one Orisha, and in others, it is said that there are as many Orisha and spirits as you can imagine plus one. In other words, no matter how much you think you know, there will always be one Orisha or spirit which you did not know about.

The purpose of the Orisha regarding the protection of humankind is to ensure that the person's iwa-pele is constantly kept in good order. The iwa-pele is seen as the goodness of the human. This natural choice between doing the right and wrong thing is what builds their axé. The axé, as mentioned before, is the life force of the person. By choosing the right decision over the wrong one, kindness over cruelty, the person's iwa-pele increases, increasing the axé. This life force runs through everything, both animate and inanimate objects, and ties the devotees to Olodumare.

Each Orisha is a saint as well. The confusion comes when people believe that practitioners worship both the saint and the Orisha; this is not the case. The saint is the Orisha or the Loa or entity and vice versa. They are the same. When devotees of Olodumare see an Orisha, they see the saint; when they see the saint, they see the Orisha. This saint-orisha-spirit transition is a perfect example of a complete syncretic religion, where the two become one completely.

Another fascinating tale about the seven powers mentioned very briefly earlier in the book incorporates the spirits of light. However, these seven powers are the seven Orishas that, when called or invoked together, will grant miracles (Fields, 2020). The seven Orishas which are used in this powerful invocation are:

- Obatala
- Ogun
- Exu
- Yemaya
- Oshun
- Shango
- Oya

Exu, Papa Legba, is the messenger or crossroad keeper and is part of the seven because he is always invoked before any ritual or invocation. If he is not summoned, he will not open the doors to the otherworld, and nothing will happen.

Before any work is to be done, it is crucial to say The

Lord's Prayer and repeat the Hail Mary three times. In some instances, the Apostles' Creed is also used. These prayers are inserted below:

The Lord's Prayer

Our Father, who art in heaven
  Hallowed be thy name.
  Thy Kingdom come, thy will be done,
  on earth as it is in heaven.
  Give us this day our daily bread,
  and forgive us our trespasses
  as we forgive those who trespass against us
  And lead us not into temptation
  and deliver us from evil,
  For thine is the kingdom, the power, and the glory,
  Forever and ever.
  Amen.

The Hail Mary

Hail Mary, full of grace
  The Lord is with thee
  Blessed art thou among women
  and blessed is the fruit of thy womb, Jesus
  Holy Mary, Mother of God, pray for our sinners
  Now and in the hour of our death,
  Amen.

The Apostles' Creed

I believe in God, the Father Almighty,
  the Creator of heaven and earth,
  and in Jesus Christ, His only Son, our Lord:
  Who was conceived of the Holy Spirit,

born of the Virgin Mary,
suffered under Pontius Pilate,
was crucified, died, and was buried.
The third day He arose again from the dead.
He ascended into heaven
and sits at the right hand of God the Father Almighty,
whence He shall come to judge the living and the dead.
I believe in the Holy Spirit, the holy Catholic church,
the communion of saints,
the forgiveness of sins,
the resurrection of the body,
and life everlasting.
Amen.

A WORD on the prayers above for those new to the Yoruba-born traditions and spiritual paths. These prayers are utilized as doorways into the spiritual realms. In contrast, it may be strange to see that there are instances where the prayers do not correlate with the belief structure of the religion. Understand that these prayers hold in them great power, and this energy is called upon when praying to them. The importance does not lie in words but in the energy that the prayers themselves hold.

Each of the seven powers is mentioned in detail below; for apparent reasons, Papa Legba is mentioned under the Loa. Each of the Orisha also has their saint equivalent. There is a prayer beneath them all and a general idea for erecting an altar in their name (Alvarado, 2009). When using the seven within your divination work, you could use something simple around the place where you choose to divine. It can be anything like a square-colored cloth representing the Orisha or Loa you wish to communicate with or who you wish to have in your divination.

In any form of communication with spiritual energies, it is

not the energy that needs to be convinced that we are communicating, but ourselves. Therefore, be as elaborate as you need to, be as simple as you need to. The Orisha are very real, very present, and ready to assist you. Be warned, though, once you have communicated with an Orisha, it is a good idea to keep the relationship healthy and strong by offering food, fruit, and alcohol where appropriate. Animal sacrifice is used in many of the Yoruba-born religions; however, no such thing is necessary for divination purposes, and I definitely do not condone any sort of human or animal sacrifice. Spirit is spirit, and within any spiritual practice, three definite laws need to be remembered in their simplest forms:

- Intention. The mere intent to work with the Orisha or Loa has created a message within the ethereal. It has set your mind into action, and you will now begin to use your perception to isolate messages from the divine.
- Focus. When divining or praying, focus is required. The mind must be stilled for the messages to come through. It does not help you to worry about what you need to do at work while you pray. You need to let go of all of that and focus on the task at hand.
- Willpower. Your willpower must be steadfast, and you must ensure that your heart and mind are working as one. There must be no fear attached to the act, and there must be a trust that the communication will work.

With these three laws in mind, there is nothing that can come between you and the act of communication. It must be said, though, that certain entities have specific desires. While many will argue that these are sometimes animal sacrifices, this is not the case. Energy is energy. While a sacrifice or energy exchange is necessary, it never has to be a life that must be given up. The raw truth is that you will feel in your gut what is needed. You will know what needs to be done, and the Orisha will communicate this. Also, try to steer clear of the more wild-of-nature spirits who have no good intentions at all. There is always an alternative route towards any goal in life. Leave such communications to those who are adept in the skill.

Nana Bukuu - The First

While many attest to the fact that Nana Bukuu or Nana Buluku is simply a primordial Orisha or the grandmother of all Orishas, she happens to be the very incarnation of the liquid waste, which is all that existed in the beginning. On this liquid waste, Olodumare created the landmass where the first humans were to live (Johnson, 2018). Nana Buluku predates the iron age, and it is said that you should never bring iron near her mound or altar.

The altar for Nana Buluku is to be kept outside at all times and never brought inside. She has been known to cause entire places to burn to the ground (Magia-Afro-Latino, 2014). Nana Buluku was the one to give birth to the sun and the moon, the twins Mawu-Lisa. It is said that Mawu and Lisa protected the slaves across the seas during the trans-Atlantic slave trade.

Altar Suggestions for Nana Bukuu

- Pink or purple handkerchiefs
- A clay vase decorated with black, purple, and pink paint for her spirit to reside in.
- A 14-day purple candle
- Tobacco
- Coconut
- Coffee Beans
- Tomatoes

- Use a clay plate for offerings
- Crown Royal Rum
- Nana Bukuu's sacred number is seven. Try to use this number in the altar decorations
- Symbols include: the angelfish, the moon and the sun, baobab trees, leaves, and sweet waters
- A bamboo knife

Note: Never bring the altar of Nana Buluku into the house. Instead, set this altar up far away from home (The Orishas: Nana Buruku, 2016).

A Prayer to Evoke Nana Bukuu

Great primordial mother of the universe. Almighty consciousness that gave birth to the sun and the moon. I call you now with reverence in my heart to hear my plea. Accept my offerings and hear the words of my heart. Assist me in knowing a solution to my problem, which is small compared to your everlasting power. I bow my head to your grace, dear grandmother of infinite wisdom.

Olokun - The Primordial Orisha

Olokun is the depths of the sea. The Orisha is androgenous, and there is much confusion in the West on whether to call this Orisha male or female. The confusion comes in when the possessions are either male or female. Olokun can be either. In some beliefs, Olokun is the parent of Yemaya; in others, Olokun is the other half of Yemaya. Olokun is never approached without a mask on. One cannot look into the face of this Orisha, or certain death will undoubtedly ensue. Olokun's name quite literally translates to the owner of the seas. Wisdom and knowledge are far beyond anything that any human or group of humans could ever wish to attain. Olokun's character is said to be mysterious, unpredictable and sometimes violent, and compulsive. Olokun is the unknown incarnate.

In a tale about a man who left his village one day to go fishing, we witness the power of Olokun and the origin of the dances. This man went fishing and was pulled into the bottom of the river, right into the depths of the sea. It was here in the cowrie shell palace where he learned the ways of the Orisha. After three years, he returned, entirely mute, to his village, which thought him to be dead. He did not stop dancing and was unable to communicate. The villagers laughed at him until he stopped dancing and could speak about the secrets of communication with Olokun to them. They have worshipped this Orisha ever since (2013).

Altar Suggestions for Olokun

- A mask of sorts, preferably white
- Terracotta pot decorated with seashells to house their spirit
- Blue and beige cloths
- White handkerchief
- Cowrie shells
- Seashell basket
- Coral
- 7-day candle

A Prayer to Evoke Olokun

Vast depths of the unknown darkness at the bottom of the sea. Divine essence who knows all and has seen the world from the beginning. Soul connected to the great Yemaya, I call you great Olokun. I ask that you accept my humble offering to answer my request for knowledge. I wish to ____(insert your plea)___. I thank you, great Olokun. My devotion to you is unstirred. My respect for you is eternal.

Note: Olokun is evoked or invoked in times of financial

hardship or when there are fertility issues. Olokun only comes to those who are absolutely clean before the altar. It is wise to have a bath before prayer in sea salt.

Saint George & Ogun

Ogun and Nana Buluku should never be evoked together because Ogun is known as the first blacksmith, and iron is detestable to Nana Buluku. Ogun is the Orisha of war, the wild hunt, and ironworking. In fact, he is iron incarnate. He is one of the more feared and revered deities in the great group of Orishas. He holds with him a scythe that can open or close any doors in the universe. Ogun is Saint Peter in Santeria and Saint George in Candomblé.

To explain the power of Ogun and his personality, think of willpower incarnate. He is the strength of everything in existence and can work through anything with great force. If you have the assistance of this Orisha, nothing can stop you, and no obstacle too big to block your path towards a goal. In his book *Myth, Literature and the African World*, Wole Soyinka, a Nigerian Nobel Prize winner, novelist, and poet writes this about Ogun: "Ogun is the master craftsman and artist, farmer, warrior, the essence of destruction and creativity, a recluse and a gregarious imbiber, a reluctant leader of men and deities" (1990).

Ogun is also one of the Orishas to bring about justice. In an old tale, if you want someone to tell you the truth or be subjected to the justice of Ogun, you must swear over a piece of iron. Ogun detests liars, and his righteousness is swift and memorable. Ogun has an entire range of spiritual entities which form part of him, in the same way as the diamond theory was explained earlier. These spirits are found only in Haitian Vodou and are known as the Nago nation (Illes, 2009).

Saint George, the patron saint equal to Ogun, is the saint

who is usually depicted slaying a dragon. Even though this imagery only appeared after the 11th century, Saint George is the patron saint who protects guards and shields against danger. Saint George is also instrumental in divination because he held dominion over stronger forces - the dragon. In some instances, it is said that Ogun is actually Saint Michael the Archangel; this is important because Saint George and Archangel Michael are prayed to together. Archangel Michael is said to have been the one who fortified the strength of Saint George and gave him the willpower to carry on.

Prayer to Saint George

Slayer of the greatest enemies, an opener of the ways, great warrior and patron saint of the people, Saint George, I call to you to intercede on my behalf. To give me the strength to move through the difficulties and the obstacles. Help me to slay my dragons in my life _____(insert your life obstacle in here)___. Through the strength of your shield, I ask for protection and unwavering faith on my path. Amen.

Altar Suggestions for Ogun

- Imagery of dogs, snakes, snails, red roosters, and crocodiles
- Ogun is usually depicted as riding on the back of a hyena or white stallion
- A calabash or eucalyptus leaves
- Red, black and green cloths
- Cigars and rum for offerings
- Nails and pieces of iron in a cauldron

Note: The altar to Ogun is usually kept in the cupboard or away from public space.

Prayer to Evoke Ogun

The iron of strength, the metal of the essence of divine power, great Orisha of the willpower of the universe, I call to you. I ask you to assist me in breaking through this problem which I have. (Speak about your situation). I ask that you guard me and shield me from the tribulations of life. Accept my offerings, great Ogun, as small as they are compared to your strength; know I give them with my heart.

Our Lady of la Caridad del Cobre & Oshun

Oshun is the personification of all flowing things. She is the beauty of the universe and blesses those who call to her with fertility and grace. She is the epitome of love and sensuality. She is also a fierce protector. While she is the smallest and slowest to anger of all the Orishas, she is the only Orisha who could fly to the creator. She has many forms, one of which is a vulture. Her sacred color is yellow, and women who wish to fall pregnant or devotees will not eat any yellow vegetables out of respect.

Oshun is the most beautiful Orisha, according to the scriptures. Appease her with sweet honey on a slice of fresh orange or sweetened milk. She provides great happiness and love to those who ask her for it. Be warned, though, do not anger her, or all hell will break loose. Oshun is also known to be one of the most generous Orisha, next to Yemaya. Oshun and Yemaya are often evoked together, but never alongside Oya.

The most popular inscription found on the Our Lady of la Caridad del Cobre statues is Mother of Charity, who walked on the road of the stormy seas. She is also known as Our Lady Charity, or more affectionately by the people of Cuba as Cachita. It is perhaps the kindness and compassion of Our Lady of la Caridad del Cobre and the kindness, generosity, and compassion of Oshun, which gives them their equal identity in spirit.

Prayer to Our Lady of la Caridad del Cobre

Great Virgin Mother, healer of the brokenhearted, giver of divine compassion for all. I call to you in this hour to intercede for me. I ask for help with ___(insert what you need help with)____. Great Holy Mother of all, I ask you to enfold me in your tender embrace and allow me to remember that there is indeed compassion and grace in the universe.

Altar Suggestions for Oshun

- Yellow, gold, and orange cloths
- Brass, copper, and gold items
- Sacred images include peacock feathers, vultures, parrots, flowing rivers, and anything which inspires beauty in you
- Always taste your offering before you give it to Oshun. She will not accept anything that is not tasted beforehand
- Honey drizzled over a slice of fresh orange is one of the best offerings you can give to her
- Mirrors, beauty products, and symbols of beauty should all adorn the altar of Oshun
- Flowers are especially welcome on her altar

Prayer to Evoke Oshun

I call to the most beautiful corner of the universe, the fastest flight, the kindest heart, *and the most compassionate flowing divine essence of existence, great Oshun. Orisha of all that moves and flows with the beauty of life. I ask for assistance in the matter of ___(insert your problem in here)___. Please accept my offering as a token of my devotion.*

Saint John the Baptist & Osain

The only Orisha to have lost one eye and one leg to a battle between himself and the other Orishas. He lost these parts of himself because he attempted world domination, and they would have none of it. Osain would have been dead if it were not for the strength and bravery of Ogun. Osain is the plant kingdom incarnate. He protects and advises all those who work with medicine and plants. He is deaf in one ear, but the other ear has hearing so acute that it can hear the opening of a flower on the other side of the universe. Ogun and Osain may be evoked together as they are powerful allies.

Saint John the Baptist is venerated as Osain. Saint John the Baptist has dominion over the healing power of all water. It is rumored that any plant which is harvested before his saints day will contain amplified magical properties. It is interesting to note that Saint John the Baptist could have been the actual Messiah, but this speculation runs into Christian opinions. The meeting space between Saint John the Baptist and Osain is the healing power that they both possess and the ability to access that healing power from the essence of the universe.

Prayer to Saint John the Baptist

Divine Saint John the Baptist, I call you to intercede for me. I wish to heal this particular situation ___(explain your situation)___. You have healed, you have intervened, and you have done what humans thought impossible. I call you now to assist me.

Altar Suggestions for Osain

- Green cloth, also accompanied by smaller pieces of red, white, and yellow cloth
- Forest botanicals, coins, and tobacco

- An iron bird
- Sacred images include roosters, turtles, parrots, and goats

Prayer to Evoke Osain

The essence of the earth, power as great as the green earth, great Orisha Osain, I call to you now to find a cure for ___(insert your ailment)___. I seek your wisdom in this matter and ask that you, who are the most knowledgeable of all Orishas about the workings of plant medicine, help me in my endeavor. Please accept my offerings to show my devotion to you.

Stella Maris & Yemaya

Yemaya is the top half of the vast oceans. She can be the violent waves or the calm, quiet sea that reveals the horizons to us. It is said that anyone who has African ancestry is automatically connected to Yemaya. It is only by her grace that the slaves who were taken across the oceans survived because of her. Those slaves who died in the journey are said to have been taken into her body. Yemaya is also the mother of most of the Orishas. She is seen as the mother of Orisha to petition for any or all issues pertaining to feminine aspects. Yemaya has many different facets, and four of these facets are:

Yemaya Asesun

Found in deep forests, Yemaya Asesun is the Queen of the Water Birds. Her color is light blue.

Yemaya Ataremawa

Also found in the forest. Still, this time in the treasures of the forests, her color is also light blue.

Yemaya Ibu Agana

This is the destructive, wrathful aspect of Yemaya. She is found at the bottom of the ocean, where it is said that she churns the destruction of that which catches her focus or calls her attention.

Yemaya Okoto

This aspect of Yemaya is the pirate sea queen who capsizes ships and drowns entire fleets. She is said to live in the seashells and sails where she likes.

STELLA MARIS and Yemaya have much in common. The nature of the mothering touch and the incredible love is shown to their devotees are just some of the personality traits they share. Stella Maris is known as Our Lady of the Stars. Yemaya has two heavenly bodies to encompass all that she is, the star and the half-moon. Stella Maris is the ocean and the lady of the stars. It is also said that Stella Maris was the star to follow across the treacherous ocean so that no one would capsize. She was said to calm the raging stormy seas.

Prayer to Stella Maris

Virgin Mother of grace, compassion, and bountiful love, I call to you in your robe of blue and white akin to the waves of the great blue sea. Great Stella Maris, mother of heavens, please help me calm the storms in my life, bring the waves to a calm ripple, and sea the horizon. Allow me divine Stella Maris to be the object of your affection through this troubled time.

Altar Suggestions for Yemaya

- Seashells, coral, seaweed, bowls of sea salt
- Sacred images include anything that resembles the ocean. Include nets, sea horses, and beach sand
- Blue and white cloths
- A star and a half-moon
- Silver objects that resemble the sea

- Seven white roses

Prayer to Evoke Yemaya

Essence of the saltwater covering the earth, potential of creation, destruction and universal grace, Mother of the vast oceans encircling the lands, Great Yemaya, I call to you. Great diviner of the waters of life, please assist me in ___(speak your heart to Yemaya, she will listen)___. I ask that you accept my offerings as a sign of my devotion to your great beauty and power.

Obatala

As mentioned in the creation story, Obatala is the universal sculptor. He is one of the Orishas who does not get angry at all. If he is disrespected, he will not retaliate. He will instead retreat to a mountain top covered in snow which is the dwelling place of Obatala. Obatala is also known as the King of the White Cloth. Everything white is his dominion.

You should never feed palm wine to Obatala because he messed up when he created the forms for Olodumare to breathe life into. He became so drunk that he created extreme deformities and strange creatures that were not according to the instructions given by Olodumare. Since that time, he has never touched palm wine again.

Altar Suggestions for Obatala

- Bones
- White cloths
- White spirits
- Milk
- Cascarilla powder
- White gold, platinum, and titanium objects that symbolize purity

- Bowls with white sugar
- White flowers

Prayer to Evoke Obatala

Great sculptor of all creation, divine creator of form, Obatala the spirit of all matter, I call to you. Please assist me in creating and forming this goal in my life ___(describe what you wish to include in your life)___. I honor your pure mastery of matter and ask that you would help me to create this in my life and intercede on my behalf that Olodumare would breathe life into my desires. I ask that you would please accept these offerings that I have presented to you, that you would see them as sufficient. I am devoted to your greatness, divine Obatala, King of the White Cloth.

Saint Barbara & Shango

Shango, like Ogun, is an alpha male within the Orisha hierarchy. It is crucial never to evoke these two Orishas together as there is a great war between them. Shango is the Orishas lover, and even though this may be the case, he is called upon to bring male virility back into a relationship or into the bedroom. He is a divinely strong competitive personality who rules over lightning, thunder, and fire.

There are many tales about the persona of Shango. Some of these tales claim that he was a living being who became an Orisha after taking his own life. Others speak of a living being who embodied the spirit of the Orisha. Shango is a generous Orisha granting great boons to his devotees.

In one tale, Shango disguises himself as Saint Barbara in order for his devotees to continue their worship of him. If there is a will, Shango will find a way to make something happen.

Saint Barbara is the great protector in times of crisis or in lightning and thunderstorms. She protects all who call to her, and her reputation bears incredible, miraculous feats. Her imagery almost always includes her with lightning in the background and a tower. It is said that she was locked in a tower even after she declared that she had sworn her virginity to Christ. Her father did not see this as pleasing and wanted her to be given over to a prince he thought would be more befitting to family affairs. Through the tales of her escape and capture, many miracles are proclaimed, such as rods becoming feathers, sheep becoming grasshoppers, and her being transported from the tower to a mountain top. Shango and Saint Barbara have become one universal entity. Unlike the other Orishas where the saints may change, this combination is universally accepted. Devotees also use the Tarot card of the tower to symbolize Saint Barbara, but not Shango, as the tower is what signifies Saint Barbara.

Prayer to Saint Barbara

Divine performer of miracles, protector of storms, and giver of grace unbounded, Great Saint Barbara, I call to thee in this hour of my despair. You know what it feels like to be closed off from the world and be saved through miracles; I ask you now to look at my situation ___(describe your situation)___ and find empathy enough to grant me a miracle out of this position that I am stuck in. Please transform my situation into ___(describe what you want the situation to look like)___.

Altar Suggestions for Shango

- Red and white cloths
- Sacred imagery include images of rams, lizards, tortoises, horses, lightning, roosters, and pheasants
- Meteorites
- Mugwort is a herb sacred to Shango
- A diviner's pestle

- Any item that is made from copper and shows strength
- A white horse figurine

Prayer to Evoke Shango

Strength and might of the tremendous storms of the universe, compassionate one who bestows great kindness on those who he favors, great Shango I call to you now. My life is in need of your power to calm the storms and dissipate the fears that are raging inside my mind and heart; please accept my offerings as a token of my devotion, and please assist me with ___ (describe your situation to Shango)___. I call you to please move into this storm and break it apart, allowing me to see the blue skies again.

Saint Sebastian & Ochossi

The place where Ochossi, the Orisha of the hunt and the forest, was first worshipped has been completely destroyed. The only known knowledge of him and how he is to be worshipped is exclusively Western. This does not mean that he never existed in Africa; it only means that the last of his devotees were either destroyed in Africa or transported over the sea. Ogun and Elegba are Ochossi's brothers, and they all live in the forest together. Ogun is said to create the iron tips of Ochossi's arrows which he tips with the most potent of poisons from his vast knowledge of plants.

The most interesting part of this Orishas' existence is not his extreme knowledge of every plant to heal and kill or the fact that he is a most potent sorcerer. He knows all that there is to know in the universe his appearance. Ochossi is a Native American or African hunter and appears as one of the two to his devotees.

Saint Sebastian's love for the people, healing, and performing miracles makes him a venerated and beloved saint in many branches of Christianity. His first death that he miraculously escaped from occurred because Emperor Diocletian found him healing people and preaching Christianity. He ordered him to be shot full of arrows. He narrowly escaped with his life. Even though he could have gone to hide from the Emperor, this former captain of the guard to Emperor Diocletian returned to heal and preach only to be clubbed to death under the Emperor's order again.

Prayer to Saint Sebastian

Oh, great Saint Sebastian, humble child of God who returns sight to the blind and works miracles wherever you go, I call to you now in this hour of need. Saint Sebastian, lover of all humanity, he who escaped death and who carries the word of God in his heart, please hear my plea of ___(speak your heart out to Saint Sebastian)___. I call to you and know that you will hear my prayer.

Altar Suggestions for Ochossi

- Green or brown cloths
- Antlers, animal hide, feathers, and any symbolism about animals
- Sacred images can include bows and arrows, the hunt, a forest, a thicket
- Offerings can consist of tobacco, peanuts, nuts of any kind, and honey

Prayer to Evoke Ochossi

Great guardian of the people, hunter, and provider of sustenance, and Orisha of justice I call to you now in this hour in which I desperately need your assistance for ___(insert your need)___. Honorable Orisha Ochossi, who survived the seas and took on the face of the new world, please accept my offering as a sign of my appreciation for your assistance.

Saint Teresa of Avila & Oya

Oya is known to be the most intellectual female of all the Orishas; she is also a warrior who presides over hurricanes, storms, and great winds. Oya and Yemaya had a run-in when Yemaya tricked Oya into taking her place in the cemetery. Instead of presiding over the oceans, Oya now oversees all matters regarding the dead. She is also thought to be the only mother of the child who is born to die. Oya's true identity is that of a water buffalo. She is a shapeshifter between this true form and her human form. She is also known to manifest as an antelope. Both Yemaya and Oshun should never be evoked or called at the same time as Oya. Yemaya, for the reasons mentioned above and Oshun, because they both share the same husband, and neither are pleased about this. Oya protects against hauntings and is a perfect ally for spirit mediums. She is usually evoked at the crossroads.

Saint Teresa of Avila was one of the most intellectual saints to have ever walked upon the earth. Through her fascinating life, she became a mystic visionary, an author whose work is still used in modern texts and psychological work, and a Church doctor. It is also said that she was the inspiration for Saint John of the Cross's work *Dark Night of the Soul*.

Prayer to Saint Teresa of Avila

The unfailing devotee of Divino Niño, remover of pain in the head and in the heart, healer of sins, great Saint Teresa of Avila, I call to you now. You who walk and commune with the angels, please hear my prayer, my life is in need of your divine guidance, ___(speak the needs of your heart to Saint Teresa of Avila)___. Divine Saint, who mapped out the interior castle to reveal the inner workings of the soul, please hear my prayer.

Altar Suggestions for Oya

- Sacred imagery may include images of the planet Uranus, a dark moon, buffalo, antelope, lightning, wind storms, or a graveyard
- Maroon and black colored cloths
- Cypress seeds, leaves, or twigs
- It is customary to have a pair of horns on the altar and summon or call to her by striking them together
- Graveyard dust
- Starfruit, nine brinjals, and red wine are good offerings to her

Prayer to Evoke Oya

Divine feminine intelligence of the universe, shapeshifter, and walker between worlds, great Orisha Oya, I call to you now. Please accept my offering as I ask you to protect me from those who wish to harm me and those I carry in my heart. I ask you great Oya, Orisha, who has seen the other side of the living, and please assist me in ___(insert your personal need)___. I ask that you show compassion for my situation and assist me as you see fit. Thank you, dear Oya.

The Spirit Allies: The Loa

The Loa all have specific rituals and offerings special to them; however, unlike the specific Orishas, the Loa are Haitian Vodou spirits who work on a particular energetic signature. Each Loa or Lwa is either a disembodied spirit or primordial energy who plays as an intermediary between the creator and humanity. Loa are not patient unless you know how to respect and work with them. It should only be the initiated or trained persons working with these spirits.

Many people believe that because Loa communicates faster in some circumstances than Orishas do, there is no harm in working with them. Knowledge is power. In the instance of the spirits mentioned herein and the vast array of Loa which are not mentioned here, one small detail could be wrong, including a thought, which will send the Loa into a shadow aspect.

The energetic signature mentioned above is like a blueprint that each of the Loa has; it is like your identity. Their identities have a frequency, and your energy must match theirs to work with them. This energetic match is acquired through correct ritual, the use of Vèvè, and sound. Coupled with that, there need to be the proper offerings and the precise amount of them, the correct timing, and the correct attire worn by the practitioner.

No uninitiated or untrained individual should ever work with the Loa. It is not only disrespectful to the religion of Vodou but also to the very nature of the spirits themselves. Humanity believes that if a spirit can change their lives, they can use them, and then there could be no harm done to them. This is far from the truth, and there are many testaments to the havoc which spirits can cause when they are disrespected or angered.

The main Loa have been entered into this book so that you are given the knowledge of their existence and what to look out for. Your divination alongside the protection and watchful eye of the Orishas is sufficient to meet the ends that you need to meet. If there is a greater interest and the Orishas show you a religious calling or path, follow it, but do not jump into the deep end before you know how to swim.

Damballah

Damballah is an infinitely large snake with approximately 7000 scales. Damballah's primordial nature means that he does not speak at all. When he mounts a devotee or practitioner, this practitioner will not talk but will hiss and spit while writhing and slithering in snake movements across the floor and up trees. It is said that Damballah originated when the world was created, and at one point, he was the only Loa. In some tales, all Loa are aspects of Damballah, precisely like in the diamond theory mentioned earlier to explain the creator. Damballah is not a god, but he is a lord of the Loa and a primordial spirit who has acquired all the wisdom of existence.

The Guédé

The Guédé family is a family of Loa who governs all aspects of death, ancestor devotion and worship, and any and all aspects of magic. Baron Samedi is the leader or head of the Guédé family and is said to heal all wounds, diseases, illnesses, and traumas. Baron Samedi has a foul mouth and is an outrageous character who drinks rum and smokes cigars. His abode is either in the spiritual realm or at crossroads where he digs the graves for those who have passed away. Until Baron Samedi digs the grave, no one is said to have died.

Marassa

The Loa Marassa is the lord of all twins. This twin Loa is revered for ruling over all dead and living twins. The symbols associated with this Loa are a 'V' shape or two eggs as a sign of fertility. It is said that possession by this Loa is not a frequent occurrence, but when it does take place, the devotee acts like a child and is then fed baby food. Twins have always held much importance in the history of African tales and culture. It is surmised that this could be traced back to the twins born from Nana Baluku: Mawu-Lisa.

Papa Legba

Papa Legba is also known by the names of Elegba and Legba. Papa Legba is the opener and closer of doorways, the cosmic doorman evoked in every ritual. He is either depicted as a child or as an old man. His wisdom and trickery are far-reaching and must be understood to communicate with the land of the dead or with the land of the Orishas or spiritual entities of the higher realms. Papa Legba stands at the crossroads.

Belie Belcan

Belie Belcan belongs to Dominican Vudú or the 21 Divisions. This Loa is an extremely important Loa who is said to be kind and compassionate. When this Loa possesses the horse, which is what the devotee is called when being possessed, the signs are a bent back right leg, a hunched over body, and a limp. A greeting will usually ensue, such as Mwen Se Belie Belcan, which translates to I am Belie Belcan. It is also said the Belie Belcan is the same spirit as Patron Saint Michael the Archangel.

The Vèvè of the Loa

The Vèvè of the Loa are like Western magical sigils. The Vèvè open doors and invite the Loa into a specific area that is contained. Each Vèvè is a map of the universe of the Loa. The Vèvè work on the subconscious mind and create a connection between the practitioner and the Loa. Vèvè are only found in the different branches of Vodou and not in the other religions in the African diaspora.

It is common to place the offerings and ritual objects on the table where the Vèvè has been drawn. Either on a piece of parchment or, more commonly, on the floor with special chalk used for the ceremony. The Vèvè is also said to communicate to the Loa through the astral and in the case of Damballah. A Vèvè is especially useful when words do not do justice for such a primordial deity. Vèvè are always used in calling down the Loa. In modern society, people have been found to save these images or tattoo them without any knowledge of the workings of the Loa that they are attached to or even if the Vèvè belongs to that Loa or not. Vèvè work on the part of the mind associated with training and initiation. They are direct invocations and invitations for the spirit to be present in your space.

FIVE

What is Divination?

DIVINATION IS DEFINED AS "THE PRACTICE OF DETERMINING the hidden significance or cause of events, sometimes foretelling the future, by various natural, psychological, and other techniques" (Park, n.d.). There are thousands of divination practices inherited and passed down through the ages from cultures across the world. In Yoruba-born divination systems, it is not simply divination that happens outside of oneself. Often the case with many practitioners. Yoruba divination systems believe that the methods which they are using are the actual embodiment of the aspects of the almighty God Olodumare.

Divination has an entire science behind it. To find an accurate equivalent to describe the position which an initiated priest in Odu Ifa holds, we would have to look at the oracles of Greece and the sibyls of Rome. To focus on a single example, we can look at the Oracle of Delphi. While the Oracles chosen as Pythia in Delphi were only women, unlike in Ifa initiation, where men and women are equal. These women would answer the questions of the people through divine intervention. The oracles were divine channels themselves who spoke the channeled words of the divine. Entire empires were built and destroyed on the words of the oracles (DeWitt & Parke, 1940).

There are many instances where divination will take place. When one is looking for a sign in life, anything that will assist you with a decision, a positive word, or a feeling is divination. When you see someone who is a prophetess, seer, priest, or priestess, you ask someone to perform divination on your behalf. And then there is self-divination. Self-divination requires a clear mind and a completely removed perception of the questions you ask. In all forms of divination, our intuition is the compass that guides us. However, in self-divination, our intuition must be the power that guides us and not our desires.

Using Your Intuition

While science is working on the predictive explanation for our intuition (Cavallo et al., 2016), let us look at what this connection with spirit actually means. Your intuition, when in sync with your guardian Orisha or any spiritual entity whom you trust and have formed a bond with, is your compass through life as well as your spiritual guardian translator in divination practices. There is no oracle in the world you can pick up and learn from if you have no connection to the spiritual world. The answers that you receive will indeed fall into the realms of scientific studies. We have a brain that is wired towards predictions. The older and more experienced we get, the better we seem to predict occurrences in life.

While this is true, we also have a spirit, soul, or Ori-Inu. This spiritual connection can only be felt when we have worked on our spiritual life and really made an effort to forge a bond with the spiritual world. Whether or not you have any inclination of divining for anyone outside of yourself or whether or not you wish to become initiated in a path, spiritual work is an integral part of our lives. It is only understood once you walk the path.

Instead of diving into divination with the logical mind, do so with the heart and mind in unison. Never perform divination without understanding the implications and laws surrounding the divination form. To illustrate the importance of this, one cannot build a building without understanding the materials needed. Where it should be built, and the size you would like to have your building be.

Another important part of intuitive language is symbolism, the back-and-forth understanding between the conscious mind, subconscious mind, intuition, and spirit, and back again. One cannot understand symbols if you have not experienced them or have no knowledge of them. This is why the study of the Odu Ifa takes many, many years to understand and integrate into an intelligible explanation to be used within readings. The subconscious mind works with symbols. This is also why each of the Loa has a Vèvè because we understand more with our subconscious mind about the universe than we do with our conscious mind.

The reason for this is the many blocks that we place in our own minds and the ever-changing perceptions we place on everything. Divination is a holistic experience of God's divine nature. The spiritual essence of all creation pulled down into matter to answer questions and give insight into everyday problems. Divining throughout your life and incorporating a system that works with you can be one of the most rewarding experiences ever. A life without the spiritual essence of life misses out on an entire universe of experience, making daily life more magical than can ever be imagined.

Cowrie Shell Importance & Divination

The cowrie shell or cowry shell, known as *Cypraeidae*, is a taxonomic family of sea snails of differing sizes. These shells have come to represent the female genitalia. However, this symbolism is a twentieth-century attribution. It has hardly anything to do with the extreme importance of the spiritual lessons found within it.

The cowrie shells were used as currency in the Yoruba tribes and across Africa and Asia. Even in Australia, shell currency was widespread; however, different shells had different values in different areas. The cowries in India, specifically Bengal, fetched one rupee for 3840 cowries. In China, the pictograph for money was fashioned after the cowrie shell. In Southeast Asia, approximately 16 grams of silver was worth one cowrie shell.

In Africa, the cowrie shells and shell currency, in general, were used well into the late 18th century. An example of how vital the cowrie currency was in Africa is the illustration of the worth of the King of Kanem-Bornu. His empire stretched across parts of Chad, Nigeria, and Cameroon. His worth was estimated at 30,000,000 cowries. Each of his adult male citizens would have to pay an annual fee of 2000 cowries for himself and his pack-ox. Furthermore, an additional 2000 cowries for every slave which was part of his household.

The spiritual reverence of these shells is found in the life of the cowrie. When it is living, it is covered by a mantle; this mantle protects the cowrie. As the cowrie adds an entirely new layer, it destroys the layers beneath to make space for the new ones. The cowrie is therefore continuously renewing itself. In this lesson, we understand the work that needs to be done to advance on our spiritual paths, as well as within our divination and devotion work. The old layers that are no longer helpful need to be surrendered and let go of. The new wisdom and information wore like a new layer to your spiritual cowrie.

Another important aspect of the divination and devotion of the Orisha and African spiritual energies regarding the cowrie shells is the importance they held for Yemaya. Yemaya is the mother Orisha who carried her people from the land they called home across the sea to where their predecessors would eventually find freedom. Yemaya is said to have stolen or been given the secrets of the interpretation of the 16 Odu Ifa and taught the other Orishas how to divine with these universal energies by throwing the cowries (Canson, n.d.).

SIX

Obi Divination

THE OBI DIVINATION SYSTEM IS THE MOST COMMONLY USED divination system among the Yoruba-born faiths. All practitioners are allowed to use the seemingly simple system regardless of initiation, status, or gender. The tale associated with the Obi divination system contains a valuable life lesson for practitioners.

Obi was a human who impressed the great Olofin. Obi was faithful and pure of heart with an outstanding level of compassion for the world around him. Olofin saw this and decided that he had the spirit to become an Orisha. Olofin bestowed this gift upon Obi. The human turned Orisha lived as a compassionate, pure, and faithful Orisha for many centuries. Unfortunately, as time went on, the continual praise and worship from devotees and practitioners grew Obi's ego. The human-made Orisha became conceited and arrogant, thinking that he was better than everything and everyone and no one could ever compare to him.

No one except the wise Ellegua could see through this arrogance. Olofin did not even hear the wisdom of Ellegua and stated that his human-made Orisha son could not be like that because he was always faithful and pure of heart. That is why Olofin had made him an Orisha in the first place.

One day Olofin threw a party for all the Orishas. Obi ensured that he would be better dressed and better looking than all the Orisha put together. And with all the effort that he put into his outfit, he even outmatched Yemaya in her blue ocean waving dress and Oshun in her magnificently beautiful honey-colored attire. While at the party, a group of beggars came to the door begging for the help of food or drink. Obi was disgusted with their filthy appearance and screamed at them to leave at once. Accusing them of being animals that belonged in the forest and not at a lavish party where the divinity of the universe gathered.

Olofin overheard this and was shocked. In his disappointment, he realized that Ellegua had been right all along, and he should perhaps have heeded the warning. When the party was done, Obi decided to outmatch even Olofin and throw a party for all of the Orishas that would be even more extravagant than his Orisha fathers had been. At this party, Obi dressed better than all the Orishas again, as well as Olofin. Obi had sent word out before the party that absolutely no beggars could be present at this party.

Despite his message that no beggars were allowed at the party, there was a knock at the door. Obi opened the door to find a terribly filthy wretched old beggar standing there and making the floor dirty. Obi screamed in disgust and slammed the door only to turn around and face Ellegua. Ellegua asked Obi why he would ever treat their father in such a disrespectful manner?

Obi realized what had happened and at once opened the door and fell on his knees in front of Olofin, who now raised his arms and allowed his axé to fill the entire room. He looked down at Obi and said that he had become a shell of the man he once was. For this reason, he would take away his ability to speak. The only way he would be able to communicate is by throwing himself at the feet of Olofin.

Olofin transformed Obi into a kola nut with a rugged exterior shell and a soft interior; the hard exterior would forever hide the interior beauty. He proclaimed that Obi would have to answer all who came to him with humbleness and truth. He then gave Obi to Obatala to work for him and all of the Orishas for the rest of time. Obatala took the kola nut and broke it into five pieces. These five pieces became the five pieces of the Obi divination.

Methods of Casting

While it is customary to divine with the Obi by using kola nuts readily available across the nations where Obi is widely practiced, coconuts have become a more respectful way of divining Obi in remembrance of the hardships and suffering that the slaves endured while crossing the middle passage.

Apples, onions, coins, and cowries are used to divine Obi. Regardless of the material used to divine with, the item must be regarded as a sacred oracle. Another factor that may be overlooked is that the diviner must be cleansed. As the oracle is cleansed and prepared through prayer and acknowledgment, so too must the practitioner themselves be washed and ready to divine.

Before divination begins, the items used for divination are to be placed on a white plate. While sprinkling cool water on them, the *Mojuba* prayer is said over them:

"*Omi tutu, ona tutu, ache tutu, tutu ilé, tutu Laroye, tutu arikú babawa. Freshwater, freshen my road, freshen my energy, freshen my home, freshen Elegguá, `Freshness that has no end, freshness so that we do not see an early death*" (Lele 200:40).

This prayer is taught to the practitioners by the priests and priestesses before divination. It is then customary to greet Olodumare in his three forms:

- Olofin - Supreme deity on earth
- Olorun - Supreme deity closest to humanity
- Olodumare - Supreme deity furthest removed from humanity

It is then customary to call on a specific Orisha to narrow down the nature of your question. For example, if you were to ask about love and if your attraction to a particular person will yield positive results, then Oshun would be your Orisha to call upon. If you had obstacles that you were facing and needed answers, then the Orisha would call Ogun into your reading.

Meanings of Divination Results

Alafia: Four Mouths Up

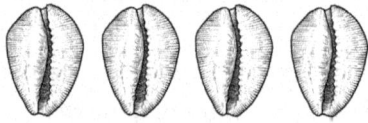

ALAFIA IN A THROW signifies that the Orishas' energies are indeed with the diviner. Depending on the Orisha present, the positive attribute will be mirrored to that strength of the Orisha.

Etawa: Three Mouths Up, One Mouth Down

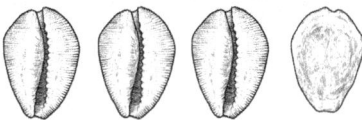

ETAWA THROWN on a first cast means that you should never ask questions you already know. However, only a hint of struggle must be overcome depending on the question because there are three mouths down and one mouth up. The light still prevails in this question, but not without warning.

On a second cast in combination with Alafia, mystery, and darkness are shrouding the question. If this is the case, the Orisha in question may have no desire to answer the question. The querent is perhaps lazy and wishes to find more accessible routes around a problem. There must be a commitment within the self when Etawa comes up in a second throw. If a third throw is in combination with Etawa, then the oracle is closed, and all that needs to be said has been said. No more questions should be asked.

If, however, Etawa is thrown and a second throw produces Alafia, then a positive outcome is on the horizon, but not before a period of struggle has been experienced and conquered.

Ejife: Two Mouths Up, Two Mouths Down

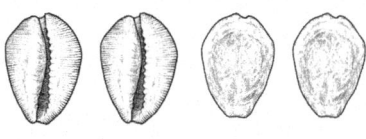

EJIFE IS the cast of balance and blessings that will be bestowed upon the diviner. A second throw is needed, and if paired with Alafia, a definite yes is given from the Orisha in question. However, the diviner or querent needs to keep up with action and dedication on their side regarding the question.

If paired with a first throw of Etawa, the outcome is still positive, and the querent needs to hold on because there is a time when the struggle ends. Ejife is the most potent combination in the Obi because of the balance aspect and will override other combinations.

Okana: One Mouth Up, Three Mouths Down

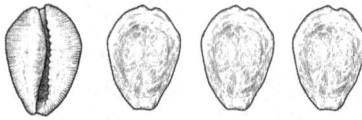

OKANA IS the cast that warns the diviner that there is a great struggle. Still, there is a tiny sliver of light within this great struggle that must be concentrated on if the diviner wishes to make it through this situation. If paired with Alafia on the second cast, then this possibility of light is amplified. The diviner must work harder to make it through the difficult times, and their thoughts must not fall away from the possibility of the light.

If the second cast of Okana is paired with Etawa, it is wise to abandon all thoughts of this question from the diviner's mind. If the second cast is paired with Ejife, then the answer is yes. The question's answer is defined as there is a struggle, but when the diviner makes it out of the darkness, it will be worth it in the end.

If, on the other hand, the second cast is paired with Oyekun, mentioned below, then all hope is lost. The answer to any question regarding the subject is a non-debatable no.

Oyekun: Four Mouths Down

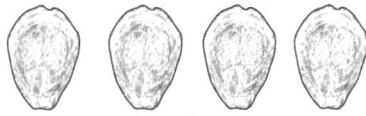

OYEKUN IS the cast that warns of all dangers and negative energies. All Obi should be cleansed and washed on a first cast. The diviner should be cleansed and washed and immediately go into prayer regarding the situation. If this same question is dared in question on the second sitting and is thrown on the first cast, then a second cast is necessary. Oyekun is the personification of negativity and when found in any reading, understand that cleansing and prayer are needed immediately. It may be wise to consult the Diloggún to assist in the following steps if you need such in-depth information.

SEVEN

Diloggun Divination

WHILE THE ORISHA ELLEGUA, WHO HAS KNOWLEDGE OF everything in the universe and is the messenger Orisha to Olodumare, as illustrated in the story of Obi, Orunmila is the second in command to Olodumare and is the Orisha with all the wisdom in the universe. As well as the Cosmic Diviner and keeper of all Odu. Odu is directly translated as chapters. However, they are much more than that which we will discuss in the methods of Diloggún.

To understand Diloggún divination, one must understand the nature of Orunmila. Orunmila, as an aspect of Olodumare himself. The three aspects of Olodumare are Olofin, Orunmila, and Olodumare or Olorun. Orunmila is the wisdom of the universe personified. In many tales, the existence of Orunmila and how he came to possess and teach the Odu varies. The Ifa which he possesses is him manifested. He embodies the very knowledge and wisdom in the sacred scriptures, which have only been an oral tradition until now. The exciting part about Odu Ifa is that it is constantly growing, and there is more being added to the wisdom (Anderson & Wilson, 1991).

As the wisdom of all the universe, Orunmila existed while the liquid waste was all that was below the dwelling place of Olodumare and the other Orishas. In fact, it is said that Orunmila was with Olodumare before the creation-thought first emerged.

In Yoruba culture, the head is the most essential part of the human. The head, which is known as the Ori, has two distinct forms. The physical head is known as Ori, and then that which is housed inside Ori is known as the Ori-Inu. Therefore, the Ori-Inu may be translated as the breath in which Olodumare gifts each human being and decides his fate and persona. The Ori-Inu is said to exist before birth, though. It also presumes that there is a decision on Olodumare and Obatala on the creation of a specific person. In other words, each person has a destiny or a reason to be alive. Life is not an accident (Lawal, 1985).

The Ori and the Ori-Inu hold such importance that it is said to be an Orisha all by itself. Olodumare placed the power and potential of Ori-Inu into Orunmila, and when this happened, intuition was born. Therefore, the Ori-Inu of every person is their intuition, soul, and connection to the creator all in one.

"Oibo, you have asked to hear our lore,
The legends of the World's young hours—and where
Could truth in greater surety have its home
Then in the precincts of the shrines of Those
Who made the World, and in the mouths of priests
To whom their doings have been handed down
From sire to son?" (Wyndham, 1921).

The lore held within the Ifa, the very personification of all the wisdom of Orunmila, is passed down through the traditions. While it has been published in many literary works today, the proper understanding of the Ifa and the many Odu belongs to the initiated priests.

To describe one such Odu, we need to look at a tale of how Orunmila escaped death, adapted for the sake of this book's purpose (Unitarian Universalist Association, 2020). It is said that Orunmila was out looking for a place to rest and settle once long ago. He found a cozy place right next to the door of Death. It seemed suitable to him, and he placed down everything that he owned onto the floor where he wished to erect his home. While he was busy making himself comfortable, Sickness, Despair, Loss, and Fight were arguing with Death to see who would go and visit Orunmila first.

At the end of a long argument, Death decided that he would visit the Orishas first. Death knocked on the Orisha's door, and Orunmila opened the door and invited Death inside with a warm welcome. When Death sat down, he offered him food and drink, and Death and Orunmila had a lovely conversation. After a while, Death decided that it was time for him to leave, and Orunmila bid him farewell.

When Death returned to Sickness, Loss, Despair, and Fight, he said that it would be best if they left Orunmila alone, and they could not believe their ears? The powerful Death had decided not to affect Orunmila? They all decided to visit Orunmila to see what Death had seen and make up their own minds. In a similar greeting, Orunmila welcomed Fight, Loss, Despair, and Sickness into his home and offered them food and drink. Sickness spoke up and repeatedly questioned Orunmila's mind and motives. Sickness tried desperately to climb into the mind of Orunmila. Still, because the intention and attitude of Orunmila were not filled with mischief or uncleanliness, Sickness was disappointed. Before the group left the house of Orunmila, Sickness ushered a stern warning to Orunmila, "You have been kind now, and we shall be on our way, but just wait. We will return one day."

Each of the Odu in the Holy Ifa contains tales such as the one above. However, they are not told like this. Like many holy scriptures found across the globe, the Holy Odu Ifa can be interpreted in many different ways.

The Diloggún works directly with the initiated priest or priestess. It takes years and years of constant spiritual work and dedication to practice the Diloggún divination system and incorporate the monumental extent of Ifa and every possible combination of the Odu into your understanding. The source of Ifa is within us as our Ori-Inu. Still, when it comes to fleshing out the entire experience and expecting you to learn in a single sitting while reading a book, it will not happen. What can happen is that the spirit of Ifa takes hold of you, and you are called to become initiated.

To understand the process of Diloggún, I have entered as much of the Odu Ifa that I can to illustrate the complexity in perceptions that can manifest depending on combinations, situations, and the querent's specific problems. I have also included suggestions from Ócháni Lele and William Russel Bascom.

Method of Reading

The Diloggún utilizes two systems within the very reading. The first and most apparent is the use of the Odu Ifa by throwing combinations of 16 cowrie shells with 16 multiplied by 16 variants, which equate to the 256 Holy Odu, or 256 holy chapters contained within Ifa. The second uses the eight ibo, which is used to determine the yes/no aspects of the querent's question and situations. The eight ibo are as follows:

Efun

Efun is the holy white powdered chalk that belongs to the cosmic sculptor, Obatala. The nature of this ibo is always positive. The powdered chalk is made finer than cascarilla powder. The object which is used within ibo is compacted enough to be able to use.

Owo

Owo is a combination of two uncut cowrie shells tied together and almost always lean towards influence from Yemaya and aspects of financial gain or loss. The Owo is almost always positive.

Gungun

The Gungun is the bone of the hind leg of the goat used to feed Ellegua. This ibo is used to answer questions about those who have passed on or any ancestral questions.

Sesan

The sesan is a negative responding ibo and is a seed from the sea-bean tree.

Ori Ere

This ibo is a symbol for the Ori of the querent. It is usually used as a tiny doll's head or a clay sculpted head that is small enough to fit in the palm of the hand. This ibo is always positive.

Apadi

The ibo of disputes, war, and chaos. This obi is made from a broken piece of a clay pot or any pottery which deems suitable.

Ota

This obi needs to be found by the diviner in the forest. It symbolizes the soul and immortality. The answer, though, is always negative but can be paired with another ibo to bring about positive change.

Aye

This ibo must be a small spiral seashell. It must fit into the diviner's hand, and it is only used in questions relating to Yemaya and Oshun.

Divination Results

If choosing to divine as an inexperienced practitioner or a non-initiate, remember that you need to have a bird's eye view perception when looking at the Odu. The combinations are terribly important. If you are too close to a situation, you may read the results completely the wrong way.

Diloggún divination also asks you to perform a few prayers. Many of which have already been outlined in the section for Obi divination. With Diloggún divination, your guardian Orisha must be called into the reading. The ancestors must be greeted and shown respect. Each person in your household must be prayed for that no harm will come to anyone and that all those living will escape death just as Orumnila did. It is then essential to set a place for Orumnila, as this is his essence that you are divining from. Further than that, take each reading slowly, and learn the meanings of the Odu Ifa.

If this form of divination calls to you, learn each of the combinations and learn their wisdom. This magnitude of life knowledge can only make you wiser in the eyes of the holy priest Orisha Orunmila. The section below will give the single throw meaning of each of the 17 combinations. Each of them will contain a short piece on the translation of the Odu Ifa where applicable or proverbs associated with the Odu and a general meaning in a reading (Oshun, 2009).

Okana: One Mouth Up

*"Where the world began by one
for there to be good, there must be bad,
where there is bad, there must be a drop of good
and where there is good, there must be a drop of bad."*

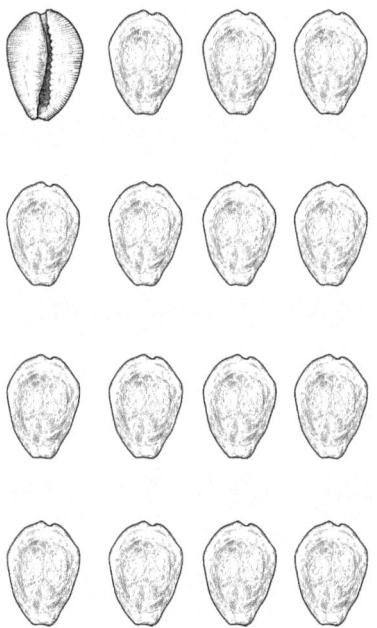

Interpretations:

- Disbelief is present
- Refrain from any crutches, substances, or negative habits
- Be truthful

- Look after your finances and do not spend recklessly
- Listen to the wisdom of the Orishas
- Find balance
- There is no answer in death
- Do not open your home to anyone
- Look after your personal life and see that everything is in order
- The querent is intelligent and independent
- The cast of divine justice

Ejioko: Two Mouths Up

"There are now arrows between brothers."

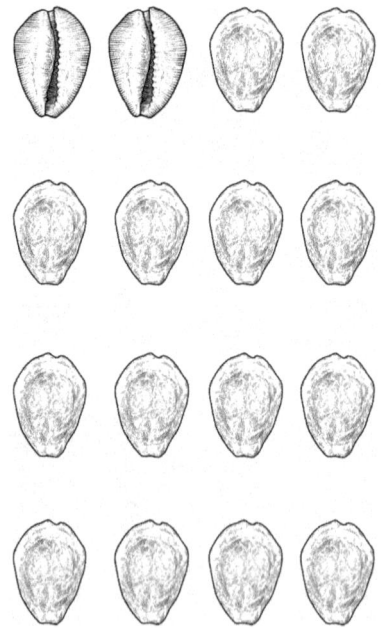

Interpretations:

- There is disagreement in the family peace must be found
- Problems concerning the law
- Someone could be twisting your words
- There is deceit somewhere in your life
- Do not bring deception into your relationships
- This is the cast of twins and triplets
- You create your own happiness and should not be looking for happiness in things outside of yourself

Ogunda: Three Mouths Up

"Tragedy over something, tragedy begets tragedy,
What has begun poorly will end badly as well.
The dog wears a vest of fire,
The leopard a vest of blood and the cat a vest of rags,
But all the animals are of the same species - that kill and eat other animals."

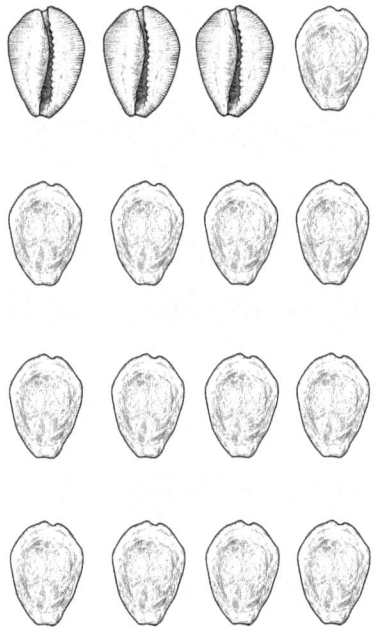

Interpretations:

- Diligent worker and strong character with the ability for great perseverance regardless of the situation
- Do not be controlled by your vices
- Hold your tongue if you think you are going to tell a secret that is not yours to tell
- Domestic violence
- Path of destruction can be turned around if you walk the straight and narrow path
- Beware of conditions about the heart
- Take time for yourself
- Control anger and rage

Irosun: Four Mouths Up

"No one knows what lies beneath the sea,
Beneath all water and land, the fires still burn.
The child born healthy and strong grows weak from lack of care.
Things unseen are sometimes best left unseen.
Open the eyes. There is much to see."

Divination with Diloggún

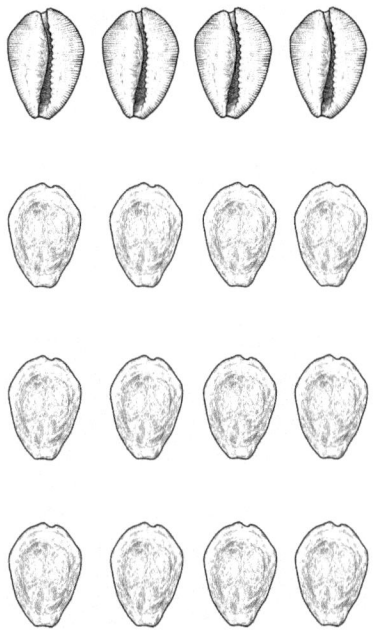

Interpretations:

- Do not be hasty to make new friends
- Look at situations from all angles
- There is something that may be hidden from view
- Beware of fraud
- Do not accept promises of repaid debt in the long run
- Within business, keep business, business and do not allow friends to pull the wool over your eyes
- Walk with your goal in your mind and do not look for trouble or alternative routes

Oche: Five Mouths Up

"Just as there are rivers on the earth, there are rivers in the veins. While your tongue is your luck, it is also your disgrace.

When we are positive in mind, all food tastes sweet, but all food tastes sour when we have a negativity in our mind.
There is a destined time for everything."

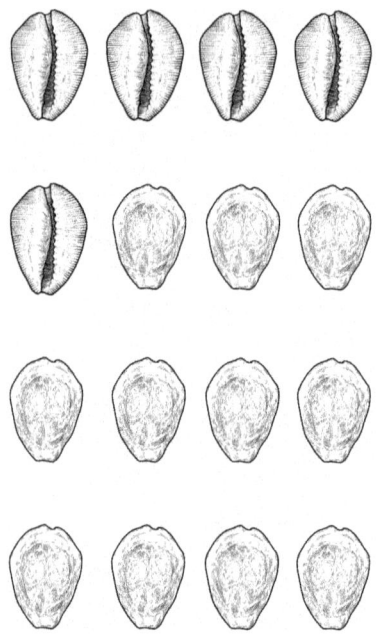

Interpretations:

- Governed by Oshun, know that she is present in the reading
- Give Oshun an offering of thanks
- The answer to the question is filled with prosperity and blessings
- Renewal of faith
- Keep your spiritual work in order
- Keep the spirits happy
- Pregnancy is a possibility
- Honor your ancestors

Obara: Six Mouths Up

Divination with Diloggún

"From legends, truths are born.
The King does not die.
You know what is truth and what is not.
Money vanishes like smoke.
From the lie, the truth shall be born.
The right-hand washes the left.
One tree does not make a forest."

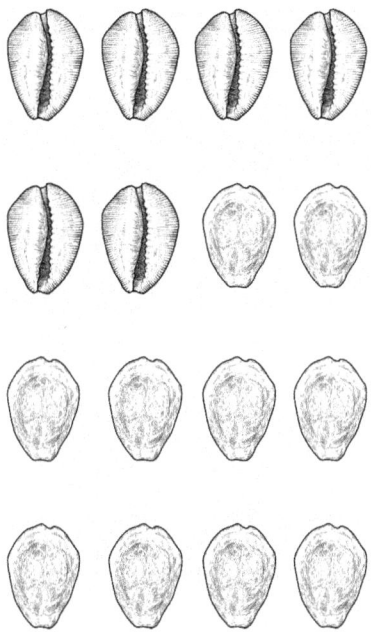

Interpretations:

- It would be wise to go for a general checkup at the doctor
- Look at your sleeping patterns
- Make sure that your mental health is in order
- Unwanted pregnancy
- Give no one a reason to gossip over your life
- Do not get into arguments with anyone
- Control the temper

- Watch your thoughts, do not let anyone get into your mind
- Eat at home

Odi: Seven Mouths Up

"The grave is finally dug.
Adultery will always bring danger.
More than luck is needed to catch the biggest fish. You will need the biggest hook in the most immense ocean with better bait than anyone.
Today it may seem small, tomorrow it will seem significant."

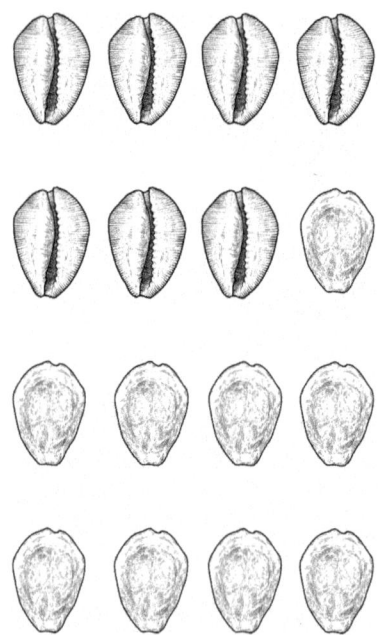

Interpretations:

- Shut the mouth, do not speak to anyone about what is in your heart
- Gossip may be surrounding the querent
- Anxiety and insomnia

- Lack of faith in the spiritual powers
- Do not take home remedies at all
- Do not try to find a quick fix to anything

Eji Ogbe: Eight Mouths Up

"It is the head that carries the body, do not lose the head.
Young palm fronds grow more vigorously than their elders do.
The biggest mistake is to not learn from your mistakes.
Do not destroy with your feet what you create with your head.
One will never desire a hat more than a crown.
To have everything is to lack all.
Where there is life, there is always hope.
Only one king can govern a town.
You will be poor when the ocean is poor."

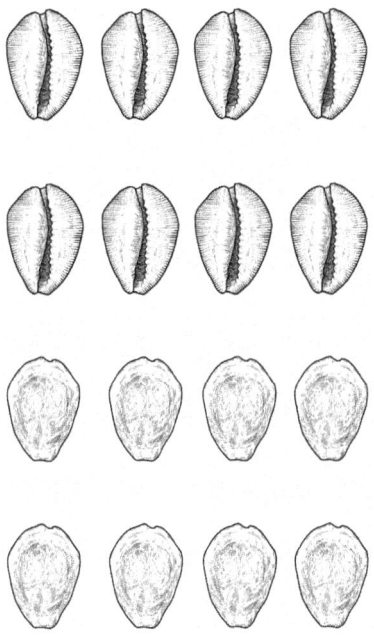

Interpretations:

- Your happiness lies in going deeper into the spiritual mysteries
- Intuitive abilities are powerful
- It is time that rebirth happens. The struggle and tears are over if humility and perseverance are used
- Put your head down, and work hard towards your goals
- Depression keeps you in your shadow
- Logic is needed to acquire balance

Osa: Nine Mouths Up

"You have left behind many things, do not attempt to recover them.
Your friend is great. The evil that he brings will be great as well.
You have many friends, yet none of them are true.
Your best friend is your worst enemy.
Change is on the horizon and approaching fast.
There is treason coming."

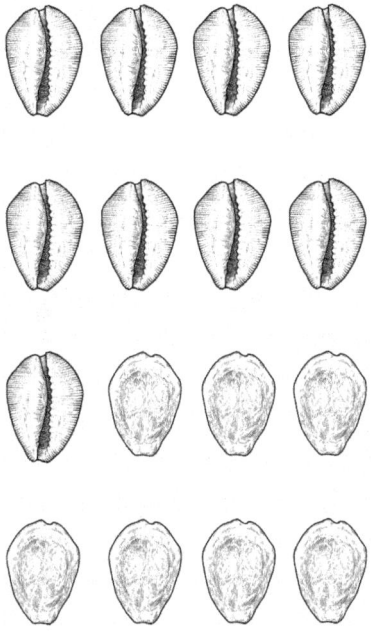

Interpretations:

- Destruction is needed before creation can occur
- Allow something to come to a natural ending
- There is a definite change, let go of everything which is not needed
- Someone or something is hiding from your view
- Your struggle will help you evolve spiritually
- Possible possession or spiritual attachment of the negative kind
- Write your ideas down if you have problems with memory
- Let the past go. It cannot serve you now. It can only cause you pain

Ofun: Ten Mouths Up

"Where the curse was born.
The one who curses shall be the one who is cursed.
Whatever is thrown into the ocean will sink to the bottom; it cannot be recovered.
Your position was lost at birth.
Odu of phenomenon."

Interpretations:

- Confusion
- Great prayer and many offerings are needed
- There is upheaval
- Robbery is possible
- Keep the home clean
- Do not try to get pregnant now
- Operations are not a wise idea at this moment, especially not cosmetic surgery

- Do not move into a new house
- A curse may have been cast
- Throw out any hoarded bottles
- Seek balance in your life at once

Owani: Eleven Mouths Up

"Ungrateful and filled with mistrust.
When water is carried in a basket, it drips between the reeds.
Water cannot be carried in a basket.
Only the coconut knows if it has worms inside."

Interpretations:

- A period of grief is foretold
- Finances will become tight
- Depression and exhaustion are foretold

- An argument could escalate and require intervention by the law
- Hidden enemies
- If the ancestors were petitioned and the deal not fulfilled the querent best make amends immediately
- The home is not a place of safety
- Keep your spiritual life and possessions safe and private

Ejila Shebora: Twelve Mouths Up

"One town must have only one ruler.
If the house is your home, you should act like the king.
The ship is sinking in rough waters.
If there is a war, you must act like a soldier, and soldiers do not sleep during battle."

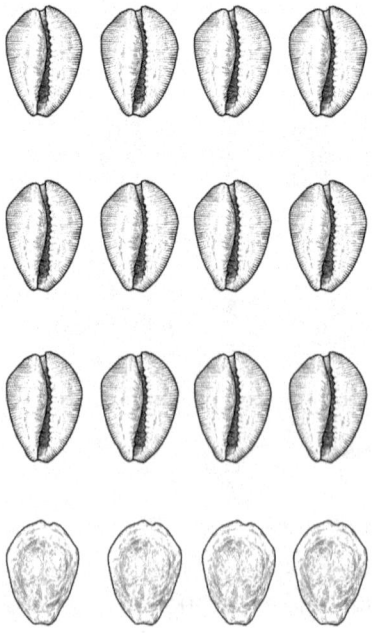

Interpretations:

- Open your eyes to see what lies around you
- Troublesome aspects in life could also become a blessing
- Never speak badly about the Orishas or about any religion
- Jokes that hurt other people's feelings or actions that make people laugh at the expense of someone else are not funny and should not be practiced
- Do not take part in family business ventures
- Do not wear patterns on your clothing

Metanla: Thirteen Mouths Up

*"Take the water from the river. You destroy the home of the fish.
Only strength can destroy evil.
The earth itself cannot fall ill.
The stone will never die.
It pays to stoop to conquer."*

MONIQUE JOINER SIEDLAK

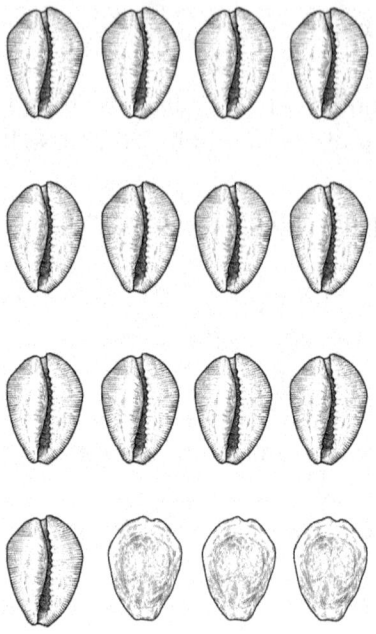

Interpretations:

- Refrain from any sort of construction work at this time
- Keep your distance from people who are ill
- Watch out for jealousy from those in a position beneath you
- Watch your back
- Do not gossip
- Affairs could take place

Merinla: Fourteen Mouths Up

"Although you have lost the battle, you have inevitably won the war.
Hot winds bring disease.
Things come suddenly, and you may miss your opportunities."

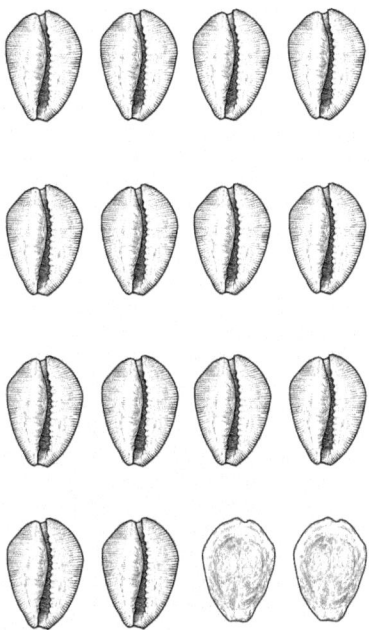

Interpretations:

- For men, there is a possible romantic interest on the horizon
- Strive with all your might to become the master and not the servant
- Use your skills
- Make use of your talents and offer them to those around you

Marunla: Fifteen Mouths Up

*"A good general does not send his best generals into battle.
Strong people work to make others strong.
Divine shrines will always be shrouded in mystery.
 My father told me to carry the bag of success on my neck, and so I will not surrender this bag of prosperity to anyone."*

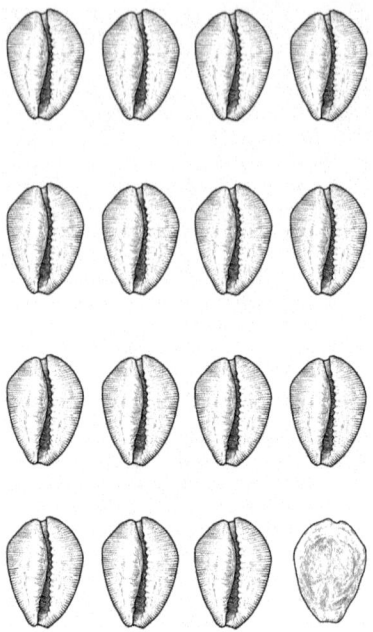

Interpretations:

- Act as if you are at war at all times, use strategy and conserve your strength for the heat at the end of the battle
- Nurture the weaker parts of your character
- There are great successes in store for the querent
- If there is a miscarriage that is known, that woman will fall pregnant soon after and will give birth to one or three healthy children
- Make an offering to Orunmila

Merindilogun: Sixteen Mouths Up

"The person you meet once, you will meet again, and you will meet him as an elder.

Patience brings great rewards.

A single holy word does more than a load of profane speeches.

Trouble comes on the day of sleeping."

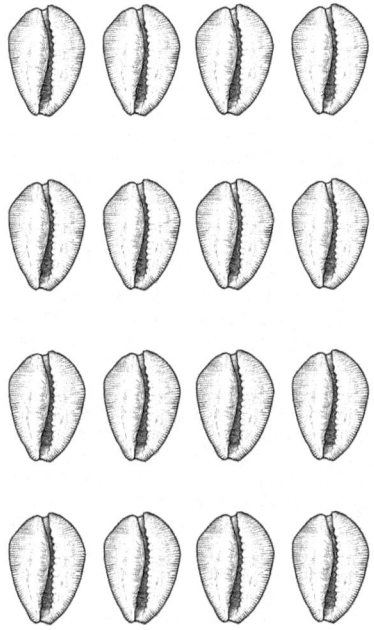

Interpretations:

- A spiritual devotion is needed throughout the life of the querent
- Words have immense power, and the querent has immense reach with their words of power
- Like the confidante to the king, the querent has the intellect and energy to change minds and lead people
- Unless the querent works closely with Ellegua, the dreams lost will remain lost, and there will never be any successes
- This querent must receive Ifa

Opira: No Mouths Up

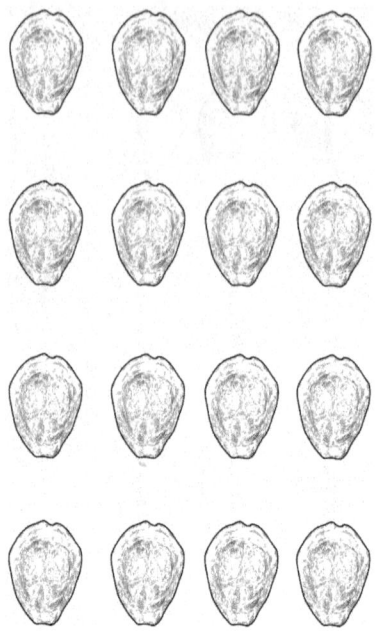

Interpretations:

- Serious issues with the reading either on the part of the querent or the diviner
- It's best to try again at a later time

EIGHT

Recipes
_____

EACH OF THE ORISHA AND THE OTHER SPIRITS ARE ALWAYS offered a plate of food. Something which will please them. The offering is a sign of respect and is imperative to any working with the Orishas. If you do not have a food offering, there are other ways to appease the Orishas, and these recipes and the food offerings, are given below. I have also added in my favorite combination for a potent floor wash that is to be used to cleanse any space of negativity. Yoruba custom is to always feed everyone in your house and then yourself; treating a spirit should be no different. All the recipes in this collection are recipes that I use. However, they are not my own and have been borrowed lovingly from many sources.

If you are in a pickle about what to serve any Orisha, look at their energies. Their specific duties and habits. Imagine whether you would see the Orisha enjoying that dish in their mind. Follow your intuition in this, as thousands of recipes are said to appease the spirits and Orishas alike. Still, then everyone believes that they have dominion over spiritual energy. Your relationship with your guardian Orisha is yours. Besides the ritual etiquette and formalities within progression towards initiation or training, you and your Orisha know what feels right for the moment. There is no hard and fast rule, significantly because many earlier recipes for offerings have been altered by passing on information through an oral method.

One thing which must be mentioned about ridding the home of negative energy is that the home should always be kept absolutely clean. Untidiness is one thing, but where filth dwells, no Orisha will show their face, especially not the seven. Laziness and sloth within your home, which is meant to be your temple, has absolutely no excuse whatsoever. Also, make sure that your body and mind are clean. Do not bring the thoughts of the day to the devotion table. If you have a problem, ask for assistance in solving it, but when you devote time to your Orisha, do just that, nothing else.

The Food Offerings

A Fruit Salad for Oshun

Nuts, flowers and delightfully sweet and orange, yellow, and golden things are sacred to Oshun. She is, after all, the Orisha of love, sensuality, fertility, and divine protection (Dorsey, 2020).

You will need:

- 3 Peeled and Sliced Peaches
- 2 Peeled and Sliced Mangoes
- ½ cup Orange Juice
- 1 ounce Peach Schnapps
- ½ teaspoon Orange Zest
- ¼t Cinnamon
- ¼ teaspoon Nutmeg
- Pinch Of Cloves

- 1 Medium-Sized Orange, Gold, or Yellow Bowl

Place all the fruit together in the medium-sized bowl. Once you have done this, combine the peach schnapps, orange juice, and orange zest in a separate cup. Combine the spices and add them to the peach schnapps, orange juice, and orange zest. Slowly sprinkle the mixture over the mixed fruit and envision Oshun in front of you when you do this. Everything is about intention. Place it in the refrigerator and remove when ready to serve to Oshun.

Hot Spicy African Chicken Stew for Ogun

In a metal dish, or alongside a piece of metal, serve this delicious Hot Spicy African Chicken Stew at the crossroads in honor of Ogun.

You will need:

- 1 teaspoon Of Cayenne Pepper
- 340g Peanut Butter
- 2 Onions, Sliced Thinly
- 3 tablespoons Sunflower Oil
- 3 tablespoons Ginger, Finely Chopped
- 3 teaspoons Ground Coriander
- 3 teaspoons Cumin Seeds
- 2 Chilis, (the hotter, the better), finely chopped and deseeded
- 2 Bay Leaves
- 400g Chopped Tomatoes
- 3 Sweet Potatoes cut into chunks
- A Handful Coriander

Begin by frying the onions in sunflower oil. Begin adding the spices, chilis, and chopped tomatoes to the mixture. Add the peanut butter and continue stirring until well mixed. Add the chicken pieces. Cook with the lid on together for approximately 30 minutes, and then add the sweet peppers to the stew. Cook on low heat for a further 30 minutes with the lid on. You can serve this dish on a bed of rice for Ogun. Don't forget to place a piece of metal alongside it.

Coconut Rice For Yemaya

Yemaya, the Orisha of the wide open salty seas, is a lover of certain foods, such as bananas, coconuts, molasses, watercress, and uncut watermelons. This recipe is an exceptionally well sought-after addition to your devotion to this Mother of all Orisha.

You will need:

- ½ cup Coconut Water
- ½ cup Spring Water
- 1 cup Coconut Milk
- 1 cup Rice
- 1 tablespoon Salted Butter

Place all the ingredients, except the rice, into a large saucepan. Cook until the water begins to simmer. Add the rice and stir continuously until all the liquid has been absorbed. Add salt and pepper to taste. Serve this dish in a blue or white bowl. Leave it on the altar for no longer than one day or offer it to Yemaya at the beach.

Nigerian Eggplant Stew for Oya

You will need:

- 2 Brinjals or Eggplant

- 2 tablespoons Oil
- ½ cup Onion, Finely Chopped
- 2 tablespoons Crushed Garlic
- 1 teaspoon Paprika
- ½ teaspoon Chili Flakes
- ½ cup Chopped Tomatoes
- 1 tablespoon Chopped Parsley

Cook the aubergine in salt water for five minutes after removing the stem and cutting it into smaller pieces. Mash the aubergine. Keep half a cup of water from the aubergine. In a deep saucepan, fry the onions in the oil. Add the paprika and chili flakes, as well as the tomatoes. Allow this to cook with a closed lid for ten minutes. Add the aubergine and cook for a further five minutes. Serve to Oya at a cemetery or, if you cannot do this safely, serve it to her at home on your altar (Olayiwola, 2021).

The Herb Pouches

A Gris-Gris Bag for Nana Buluku

In a small pouch of navy blue, blend the following herbs and leave them at the crossroads (Dorsey, 2017).

Spanish Moss

- Garlic
- Juniper berries
- Sage
- Cypress
- Tobacco

Do not ask Nana Buluku for anything unless you are initiated. Instead, do this as a way to honor her primordial energy and vast wisdom.

A Gris-Gris Bag for Oya

This gris-gris bag is handy for spirit mediums and those who work with Oya. The pouch itself needs to be made of strong charcoal-colored material. The herbs to add to the bag are:

- Horehound
- Patchouli
- Comfrey
- Chickweed
- Dittany of Crete
- Dragons blood
- Nutmeg
- Oakmoss

Leave the bag for Oya at a cemetery or on your altar. If you are leaving her this bag to honor her, do not fetch it. If you are using it as a connection with her and a protection bag from her as your Orisha or as an amplifier in your workings, then retrieve it. Thank her and wear it on your person until you feel that a new one is needed (Myoruba, 2014).

Floor Washes

Floor Wash to Dispel Negativity

You will need:

- Cascarilla powder – also known as powdered eggshells
- 7 drops of myrrh oil

- 7 drops lemon balm
- 1 teaspoon sea salt
- 1 cup spring water
- 7 spearmint leaves

This floor wash can also be used in a misting bottle and sprayed into the corners of the area you want to cleanse. Once you have mixed all the ingredients together, stir well and allow to sit for one hour. Strain the floor wash through a piece of cheesecloth. Use the mixture within one day of making it. Do not keep it, as it will go off (Dorsey, 2020).

NINE

The Medicine of the Yoruba

WITHIN THE IFA CORPUS ARE THE REMEDIES TO ALL ILLNESSES and the use of the earth plants for healing and expelling the spirits that cause infections. These spirits are known as ajogun. The only mission of these spirits is to generate an imbalance in all of humanity to be strengthened and uplifted.

Science has only begun to understand what the Yoruba people understood about the energy of all life. It is when this energy is disrupted that illness, sadness, despair, and disease occur. Unfortunately, when it is already manifest in the body, it takes a lot of work on the medicine healer and the person being treated to restore health.

One Orisha, which we did not cover in the above section on the Orishas and saints, is Erinle. This is because he belongs wherever the medicine of the green earth and the very essence of all the natural world is. This Orisha lives in the forest along with his brothers, Ochossi and Ogun. He is the sheer strength of the wilderness. He knows the voice and spirit of each plant and how to heal or kill with them all. The Yoruba people understood the duality of this world. In this understanding, know that Erinle would need a positive and negative side. He is known as the elephant of the world. However, as nature changes, so can he. If he needs to be the flowing water, he is transformed into his feminine healing form. If he needs to be the natural land, he is Erinle in all his strength and unbridled power.

Without understanding the spiritual connection to the creator and all life around you and a deep reverence for the energy within the earth, it is quite impossible to understand the magnitude of healing that occurs through plants and the energetic signature they carry. However, suppose this has been understood, and you have a deep affinity for healing. In that case, Erinle will teach you about the various combinations with which any illness, trauma, and pain can be healed. Remember that Erinle must be seen as an energetic field in the universe. It permeates through the energy of a specific Orisha or plant energy to affect healing within the ax of the person, which then causes change within the actual body. It is impossible to change matter. However, it is very possible to change the energy which creates the matter.

The following correspondences work in unison with Erinle. He must be called with the Orisha needed to provide the precise healing necessary.

Obatala: The bones, all white fluids, the brain
Elegba: Parasympathetic nervous system, sympathetic nervous system
Yemaya: Liver, breasts, buttocks, and womb
Oshun: Digestive organs, female genitalia, circulatory system
Ogun: Tendons, sinews, kidney (adrenal glands), and the heart
Shango: Male reproductive system, life force, bone marrow
Oya: Breathing, bronchial passages, mucous membranes, lungs

In all aspects of healing, regardless of how the healing occurs, there is a search for homeostasis. This perfect state is not a myth if we understand the forces at play. There needs to be a good solid understanding of science and ancient practices, which sometimes are light years ahead of science.

When looking into the Egyptian understanding of the various elements and how the entire cosmos is composed, we find that the Yoruba correlation is almost the same. Instead of an element, the Yoruba teachings provide an Orisha. The elements and Orishas are:

Yemaya: Water - West - Cold and Wet
Shango: Fire - North - Hot and Dry
Erinle: Earth or the energy force of the human being - South - Dry and Cold
Oya: Air - East - Hot and Wet

Each element has its corresponding direction, and so do the Orishas. On top of this understanding, each element within nature has a light and dark aspect. In the Yoruba tongue, this would be described as hot and cold, wet and dry.

Every herb has a governing Orisha and therefore takes on the aspects of the Orisha. So, the Orisha and the plant share their energetic signature. The Orishas and some of the herbs that they govern are mentioned below:

Obatala: sage, skullcap, kola nut, hyssop, blue vervain, white willow, valerian
Oshun: burdock, cinnamon, yarrow, chamomile, lotus, buchu, myrrh, echinacea
Yemaya cohosh (blue and black), dandelion, aloe, spirulina, passion flower, wild yam root
Ogun: alfalfa, hawthorn, parsley, motherwort, garlic, eucalyptus, and bloodroot
Oya: mullein flowers, comfrey, elecampane, horehound, chickweed

Shango: plantain, hibiscus flowers, stinging nettle, cayenne pepper

Many people have their own ideas about which herbs and plants belong to which Orisha energies and how to heal their clients. This is perfectly alright, as healing is simply energy work. Because we are all unique and created from the sacred clay through the vision of Obatala, we all have a different method or tiny tweaks of how our own spiritual connection works.

Religion messes things up sometimes and dictates what is right and what is not. While this is necessary for the work of such delicate information, it also makes many people retract from their paths of becoming healers or diviners. It is said that you are either a healer or a diviner. This is absolute nonsense. You can be both, and many people are. However, the work required is immense and takes all your life to master. Like the monk who dedicates their life to the monastery and sacred practices, giving up all known material attachments, so too does the path of the healer and the diviner call the devotee to surrender all known attachment so that Olodumare and the universal secrets can be learned.

When you travel further into the mysteries, you will understand that many paths are precisely the same. The only difference is that the African Yoruba-born understanding of the universe is the oldest. There is an old Toltec tale of the beginning of Atlantis. How the fathers or elders of the tribe saw the egotistic destruction of the people. They called a secret meeting. Each of the elders agreed to take a version of the great truth that would give humanity all the power in the universe to the furthest corner of the world. This tale explains why the cultures worldwide hold the same tales as each other but with slight differences and changed names. If Africa is the oldest surviving understanding of the universe perhaps, Africa contains the truth of the universe (Staff, 2018).

TEN

The Importance of Prayer

Disregarding everything else in the world except our own skin, mind, and axé, we have only prayer to communicate. In this raw imagery, we understand the importance of prayer in forging a connection with the divine. Setting aside time to spend in the spirit of your guardian Orisha and the very essence of being is the most important and vital first step in doing anything in the Yoruba-born religions or ways of life.

Prayer is not simply a prerequisite within the sacred texts. Prayer is a divine morse code of vibration that communicates your innermost truth to the universe and to the heights of Olodumare himself. There is such power in prayer that it is often said to move mountains. Prayer is also not a Christian or monotheistic, Santeria, Islamic, or Yoruba-religion thing. It goes far beyond that. Prayer is not even words or mindfulness. It is more than that.

Prayer is sitting in the space that you have made sacred or just in the area where you find yourself right now. It is surrendering your heart and your Ori-Inu up to the heavens through the seven lines. Beyond time and human understanding and existing in the realm of God himself. Prayer is what is used to heal. It is prayer that calls the Orishas to come and join you in the ritual. It is prayer that changes the odds of one's Odu, and it is prayer that brings the message into matter.

Above and beyond the prayers added to the various Orishas and saints in this book. They are used within Catholicism but have deep significance within Santeria as well.

The Prayer of Jabez

"Oh that you would bless me indeed, and enlarge my territory, that Your hand would be with m, and that You would keep me from evil, that I may not cause pain" (Prayers, n.d.).

Prayer to Holy Saint Michael the Archangel

"Holy Michael, the Archangel, defend us in battle. Be our safeguard against the wickedness and snares of the devil. May God rebukes him, we humbly pray, and do you, O Prince of the heavenly host, by the power of God cast into hell Satan and all the evil spirits. They wander through the world, seeking the ruin of souls. Amen" (Prayers, n.d.).

The Prayer of Jesus at Gethsemane (Olofi)

"Father, if you are willing, take this cup away from me. Nevertheless, let your will be done, not mine" (Prayers, n.d.).

Canticle of Brother Sun and Sister Moon of Saint Francis of Assisi

"Most High, all-powerful, all-good Lord, All praise is Yours, all glory, all honor, and all blessings.

To you alone, Most High, do they belong, and no mortal lips are worthy to pronounce Your Name.

Praised be You, my Lord, with all Your creatures,
especially Sir Brother Sun,
Who is the day through whom You give us light?

And he is beautiful and radiant with great splendor,
Of You Most High, he bears the likeness.
Praised be You, my Lord, through Sister Moon and the stars,
In the heavens, you have made them bright, precious, and fair.
Praised be You, my Lord, through Brothers Wind and Air,
And fair and stormy, all weather's moods,
by which You cherish all that You have made.
Praised be You, my Lord, through Sister Water,
So useful, humble, precious, and pure.
Praised be You, my Lord, through Brother Fire,
through whom You light the night, and he is beautiful and playful and robust and strong.
Praised be You, my Lord, through our Sister,
Mother Earth
sustains and governs us,
producing varied fruits with colored flowers and herbs.
Praised be You, my Lord, through those who grant pardon for love of You and bear sickness and trial.
Blessed are those who endure in peace. By You Most High, they will be crowned.
Praised be You, my Lord, through Sister Death,
from whom no one living can escape. Woe to those who die in mortal sin! Blessed are they She finds doing Your Will.
No second death can do them harm. Praise and bless my Lord and give Him thanks,
And serve Him with great humility" (Canticle of Brother Sun and Sister Moon of St. Francis of Assisi - Prayers, n.d.).

Ancestor Prayer - To be used when Offering Libation

"Omi tutu
 Ona tutu
 Ile tutu
 Tutu Laroye
 Olodumare, Olodumare, ajuba gbogbo iku t'e'mbe'l'ese Olodumare,

iba ara t'orun."
   English Translation:
   "Cool water
   Cool road
   Cool House
   Cool speech
   Olodumare, I praise and salute all the ancestors who sit at your feet. I praise and salute all of heaven" (Oshun, 2016).

ELEVEN

The Concept of Death

DEATH IS EITHER A TRAGEDY OR A CELEBRATION OF REBIRTH IN many cultures across the world. In Yoruba religions, death is seen as a movement from one place to another. The tales tend to differ depending on the belief of the practitioner and their level of devotion to any particular Orisha. The movement surrounding death worship, which may not be found to be a Yoruba-born tradition, is still included within the 21st-century perception of many Afro-Latino worshippers.

As in Yoruba, death perceived without outside influence is seen as a moving of house from the land of the living to the land where the disembodied souls live. In other tales, it is a movement of the axé into the guardian Orisha of the deceased. Within the Yoruba teachings, Death and Sleep entities are seen as siblings; Death is the eldest of the two. There are many reasons why Death sends to fetch the heart or axé of the person. These reasons include sickness, loss, stupidity, accident, and litigation.

The original design of the universe was not to include death. The forms created by Obatala were meant to live on forever. This immortality was given to the frog to guard, and instead of giving it to the people, he used it for himself. This is why the frog can feel no pain. However, this has since been scientifically proven to be wrong. Frogs do, in fact, feel pain (Guénette, 2013).

Within the burial rites of the Yoruba people, the ghost is said to hover around if it is found that the axé is not taken up by the guardian Orisha. In this case, the relatives understand that the poor soul must be cared for and will choose through the divination of Odu Ifa, a woman who takes care of the disembodied spirit. She will sit on the grave or near the body, and every time she eats, she will offer the same portion of food to the spirit of the deceased.

One notion of reincarnation in the ancient Yoruba way was that of returning spirits. The axé of the person would cycle through life, death, and rebirth repeatedly. The important part to understand here is that much of reincarnation happens within the family line. Therefore a mother could give birth to her deceased great uncle or, even more recently, her deceased mother or father. Every child born is divined over to see who this child is and whether they are reincarnating the family line or a stranger. This stranger can be the axé of an animal, plant, or spirit which inhabits the river or anthill. Depending on the nature of the child's reincarnation, they are named as such. In other words, if you give birth to a child, and that child is found through Odu Ifa, that it is, in fact, your deceased mother's spirit reincarnated, it will be named, *Mother returns* (Olomola, 1988).

On the other side of the world, a 21st-century ideological shift has occurred, potentially changing how death is viewed within Yoruba religions. The cult of the folk saint, Santa Muerte, is the "single fastest-growing new religious movement in the Americas" (Chestnut, 2017).

Santa Muerte's reputation has not been a pleasant one, and she has been known to be the consort of those who are on the wrong side of the law. In the past, her masculine identity was the only sign that God loved the criminals as well. Today,

Santa Muerte advocates for many Hollywood releases, people who find themselves controlled and stuck in the ways of an oppressive society and the LGBTQ+ community (Chestnut, 2017).

Saint Santa Muerte has been rejected by the church. She has brought fear into the people who do not understand the inner workings of the concept of death, but at the same time, she has breathed life into the old ways of saint worship. Her stance is strong, and she guards those who dare to interrogate, defile, abuse, or deface any other human being. She stands firm in protecting those who are hopeless or do not have a voice to speak out in the world. Saint Santa Muerte has given death a female persona in line with the original feminine energy of the moon twins mothered by Nana Buluku. She has brought strength and a language with her that the people of the twenty-first century speak. There is always change in the world. The change instilled to combat fear, rejection, and disempowerment is a change of death. Death is symbolic, and the fear that this folk saint brings out in many people is for nothing. She provides strength to her devotees. She allows them to experience life without the struggle of simply being an outcast.

A Prayer to Saint Santa Muerte

"Divine feminine personification of death bearing sainthood for the feats of freedom that you have shown, Santa Muerte, I call to you now! Hear me in this time of struggle, isolation, and fear. Bring death to the pain, leaving space for new life to be nurtured and grow. I ask specifically that you please remove the following ___(insert your specific problem)___. This issue needs a quick death, and I have full faith in you, great Saint of the people. Amen."

Altar Dressing for Saint Santa Muerte

- A votive candle representing a female, a skeleton, or a hooded figure carrying a scythe
- A dark-colored altar cloth of your choice
- Tequila or rum
- Tobacco in a pipe or cigarettes
- A glass of spring water
- A small round mirror

Pan de Muerto (The Bread for the Dead)

This bread is made for the feasting weekend of Dia de Muertos or The Day of the Dead in Mexico. This bread can also be offered to all those who dwell on the crossroads (Dorsey, 2020).

You will need:

- ¼ cup Shortening or Corn Flour (add unsalted butter if you use corn flour)
- ¼ cup Milk
- ¼ cup Warm Water
- 2 cups Baking Flour
- 1 cup Bread Flour
- 2 tablespoons Sugar
- ½ teaspoon Sea Salt
- 2 Eggs

Melt butter and cornflour or shortening in a saucepan. When this is completely melted, add ¼ cup of milk. Allow this to simmer, and then pull it off the stove. Add your warm water. In a separate bowl, combine all the dry ingredients together. Begin by adding the dry ingredients to the wet ingredients, do this slowly. Mix thoroughly, and then add the 2 eggs. Once you have mixed everything together and it does not stick on the side of the saucepan, you are ready to use your imagination and shape your bread.

Once you have done this, bake for 20 - 30 minutes at 350 degrees.

To make peace with death if you fear it or have suspicions about life after death, highlight instances in your past where sudden death has occurred. Not in the true sense of a person, but there was a sudden change in situations where there was a sudden change for no apparent reason. This could be the moving of house, a friend who all of a sudden stopped talking to you, or you had a sudden feeling that you should end something immediately. This ending, this change, is the spirit and essence of Death.

Death should be revered, not feared. Death is something that no one can escape and something continuously referenced in the Ida Ifa and in every corner of the globe. It is the one power, the one Orisha, which holds sway over everything and everyone. An ingrained Western concept believes that speaking to the dead or communing with the spirit world is evil. The practitioner would be damned to a hell worse than their imagination if they were to perform anything of the sort. Unfortunately, this fear is in the subconscious mind. It is portrayed in movies, in the media, in our literature, and in daily news. Holding elaborate funeral ceremonies is seen as ridiculous and belonging to the mind of radicals.

Death is real. She is awake, and she is here to effect change in the world of humankind, believing that they have controlled the reigns for far too long. There is also a great peace in allowing death to do what she does best: inflict change of perception. There are only two instances where a person is ripped from their sanity, that is, in the face of love and death. Speaking to our departed loved ones may be part of our religious practice, but it is also part of humanity. It is something that unites us. If we learn to understand ourselves and the world around us, death is no longer feared, nor is it something that even bothers the mind. It simply becomes another step in the experience of being human. Many helping hands lie in the understanding of Oya and Saint Santa Muerte worship. There are also many blessings waiting around the corner when you forgive, heal and bless your ancestral line. This importance is why the ancestors are never forgotten or left out of any ritual or devotional practice. If you feel hesitant to devote an altar to your ancestors, simply speaking to them as though they are right next to you will bring you much healing. Perhaps silence the fears and misconceptions about death and the life hereafter.

Conclusion

Africa may lie in the soul of every being on earth. Her tales have traversed lands, crossed oceans, and buried themselves inside every spiritual path. Perhaps the similarity is the will of the divine. Maybe the Loa have decided to play cat and mouse with the Ori of humanity. Maybe this is a question better left unanswered.

The delicate manner in which we approach our life begins and ends with a single thought. There is a continuous Ori-Inu within the cycle that every human experience throughout their lifetimes. The path you choose to discover the language of your soul is a lifelong journey, but each decision has ramifications. It is unwise to believe that matter has precedence over spirit. Thankfully, scientists can show us with multiple experiments that everything is indeed energy.

It is unknown when the Ifa Odu was first spoken in the tongue of the Yoruba people or when the first cowrie shell replaced the kola nut. Still, the mathematical precision and unbelievable wisdom in every single Odu without combination is enough to provide a long and happy life. When we attach the combinations to their knowledge, without even divining, but simply meditating on the words of Orunmila, the

Conclusion

essence of Ifa, we have a definite path to what is called Nirvana in the East.

The Yoruba religions provide the ancient blueprint to the connection and reconnection of humanity to spirit. The onus is on the human being to look after their own actions and thoughts, mind their desires for material attachment over spiritual work. There is a great sense of belonging formed in the mind of any of the Yoruba religious devotees, one which is not readily broken or destroyed. This is because of the peace of understanding all lives as one. There is one creator devoid of gender. Whether they are rich or poor, whether they have a college degree or have been eating out of the dustbins for the last week, each person contains the same spirit of God, which gave them life.

There is no discrimination under the watchful gaze of Olodumare. Without gender, removed from duality, this creator stands as the sky above us. The personification of the very heavens that we gaze at with longing in our hearts. The golden chain is still hooked into the sky, and the seven powers or seven lines are there to be understood, revered, and respected.

The hunt for personal power within oneself is paramount to the journey ahead. When we venture into the realms where personal power is sought to control any spirit, Orisha, or fellow human being, then we have the entirety of spirit from the beginning of time watching us. Knocking at the door and demanding that penance be paid upfront. No ill deed is ever overlooked under the authentic Yoruba way. There is law and order to the universe. Each thought that passes through your mind has consequences within your life.

It is human nature to believe that more power is better. Collection of material possessions will make the Orishas love you more. It is common to see the altars of some people adorned with a thousand more items than is necessary. The intention and the devotion in your heart is the key to

Conclusion

unlocking the presence and wisdom of your guardian Orisha. You do not need to afford all the candles, scrubs, and herbs at once. Be patient with your practice and find stillness in the path. There is no rush. We all return somehow, somewhere. The eternal cycle is believed to never end until Obatala decides he will no longer fashion new reflections of himself in the water or when Olodumare decides that he will no longer breathe life into the forms or into the earth itself.

You are the very essence of the creator. Due to the material illusion clouding your head, you have perhaps forgotten that your origin is from the sky. You have possibly forgotten that your mother is the waves and that your breath is holy. The breath controls life. When it is taken away, you are simply a clay figure formed after a mirror image of God.

Divination with Diloggún was written with all humanity in mind, with the history of the Yoruba people in heart and the spirit of the creator breathing into the pages. Spirituality can get tricky. It can mess with the head, which is why Ifa says protect your head constantly. Never allow anyone to tell you what is more important if you know the truth in your heart. Never give away your control of your own mind to any other human being, it belongs to you, and it is your gift. Always remember that this path is your path to return to the creator. This is your path to perhaps become a better man-turned-Orisha than Obi ever was.

Happy Divining!!

References

Africa Update Archives. (n.d.). Africa Update Archives. Retrieved May 9, 2021, from https://web.ccsu.edu/afstudy/supdt99.htm

Allen, H. L. (1970, January 1). A diverse continent: African textiles in context exhibition opening May. Global Health Institute. https://ghi.wisc.edu/a-diverse-continent-african-textiles-in-context-exhibition-opening-may/

Alvarado, D. (2009). A guide to serving the seven African powers. Createspace Independent Pub.

Anderson, D. A., & Wilson, K. A. (1991). The origin of life on Earth: An African creation myth (1st ed.). Sights Production.

Animal sacrifice in Brazilian folk religion. (n.d.). ScienceDaily. Retrieved May 9, 2021,https://www.sciencedaily.com/releases/2009/08/090825203332.htm

Beres, D. (2019, January 30). The origin of humans is not East Africa. It's much broader. Big Think. https://bigthink.com/21st-century-spirituality/the-origin-of-human-beings-is-not-east-africa-its-much-broader

Black, R. (2010, April 19). The history of air. Smithsonian

References

Magazine. https://www.smithsonianmag.com/science-nature/the-history-of-air-21082166/

Buenfeld, S. (2020, August 7). Spicy African chicken stew recipe. BBC GoodFood. https://www.bbcgoodfood.com/recipes/spicy-african-chicken-stew

Canson, P. E. (n.d.). Yemonja - Yoruban deity. Encyclopedia Britannica. Retrieved May 11, 2021, https://www.britannica.com/topic/Yemonja

Canticle of Brother Sun and Sister Moon of St. Francis of Assisi - Prayers. (n.d.). Catholic Online. Retrieved May 12, 2021 https://www.catholic.org/prayers/prayer.php?p=183

Carol J. Williams. (2018, September 4). In Haiti, voodoo gets official recognition. Chicagotribune.Com. https://www.chicagotribune.com/news/ct-xpm-2003-08-05-0308050313-story.html

Cavallo, A., Koul, A., Ansuini, C., Capozzi, F., & Becchio, C. (2016). Decoding intentions from movement kinematics. Scientific Reports, 6(1). https://doi.org/10.1038/srep37036

Chesnut, A. R. (2017). Devoted to Death: Santa Muerte, the Skeleton Saint (2nd ed.). Oxford University Press.

Chestnut, A. (2017, February 17). Sex & Death: Santa Muerte's Strong LGBT Following. Death & the Maiden. https://deadmaidens.com/2017/02/15/sex-death-santa-muertes-strong-lgbt-following/

Chiorazzi, A. (2015, October 6). The spirituality of Africa. Harvard Gazette. https://news.harvard.edu/gazette/story/2015/10/the-spirituality-of-africa/

Comparing biographies of enslaved Africans from different regions. (2020, November 17). [Video]. YouTube. https://www.youtube.com/watch?v=JUYbn2Zi4yU

Crash course Medieval Africa. (2018, February 21). [Video]. YouTube. https://www.youtube.com/watch?v=qG-iLiKPm5Q

Creation stories. (n.d.). Railsback. Retrieved May 11, 2021, from http://railsback.org/CS/CSGoldenChain.html

References

De Armas, D. (n.d.). Things you should know about: Santería. Latino Life. Retrieved May 9, 2021, from https://www.latinolife.co.uk/node/231

DeWitt, N. W., & Parke, H. W. (1940). A history of the Delphic Oracle. The Classical Weekly, 33(17), 201. https://doi.org/10.2307/4340860

Dorsey, L. (2016, August 15). Recipe: Yemaya coconut rice. Voodoo Universe. https://www.patheos.com/blogs/voodoouniverse/2016/08/recipe-yemaya-coconut-rice/

Dorsey, L. (2017, January 28). Nana Buruku: Warrior, wisewoman, and goddess. Voodoo Universe. https://www.patheos.com/blogs/voodoouniverse/2017/01/nana-buruku-warrior-wisewoman-and-goddess/

Dorsey, L. (2020). Orishas, goddesses, and Voodoo queens: The divine feminine in the African religious traditions. Weiser Books.

Elliott, M., & Hughes, J. (2019, August 19). A brief history of slavery that you didn't learn in school. The New York Times Company. https://www.nytimes.com/interactive/2019/08/19/magazine/history-slavery-smithsonian.html

Engler, S. (2012). Umbanda and Africa. Nova Religio, 15(4), 13–35. https://doi.org/10.1525/nr.2012.15.4.13

Equiano, O. (2000). By Olaudah Equiano - The Interesting Narrative of the Life of Olaudah Equiano, or Gustavus Vassa, the African, Written by Himself. W. W. Norton & Company.

Fields, K. (2020, January 18). The seven African powers for beginners (African spirituality & magic). Otherworldly Oracle. https://otherworldlyoracle.com/seven-african-powers/

Fischetti, M. (2015, June 16). Africa is way bigger than you think. Scientific American Blog Network. https://blogs.scientificamerican.com/observations/africa-is-way-bigger-than-you-think/

References

Guénette, S. A. (2013). Pain perception and anaesthesia in research frogs. PubMed. https://pubmed.ncbi.nlm.nih.gov/23615302/

Guynup, S. (2021, May 4). Haiti: Possessed by Voodoo. Culture. https://www.nationalgeographic.com/culture/article/haiti-ancient-traditions-voodoo

Harvey, M. (2015). Deity from a python, earth from a hen, humankind from mystery: Narrative and knowledge in Yorùbá cosmology. Estudos de Religião, 29(2), 237–270. https://doi.org/10.15603/2176-1078/er.v29n2p237-270

Herbstein, M. (n.d.). African religion and Candomble. AMA Africa Today. Retrieved May 9, 2021, from http://www.ama.africatoday.com/candomble.htm

Herren, V. (n.d.). I.W. Articles. Go Heathen. Retrieved May 10, 2021, from https://www.goheathen.org/articles/diamond.html

HomeTeam History. (2018, February 14). Africa's most significant events: A timeline [Animated] [Video]. YouTube. https://www.youtube.com/watch?v=NZ9WIhu5sG8&feature=youtu.be

Idowu, B. E. (1995). Olodumare: God in Yoruba belief (2nd ed.). A & A Book Dist inc.

Illes, J. (2009). Encyclopedia of spirits: The ultimate guide to the magic of saints, angels, fairies, demons, and ghosts (1st Edition). HarperOne.

Johnson, E. O. (2018, July 31). Nana Buluku, the revered goddess and supreme deity of West Africa and the Caribbean. Face2Face Africa. https://face2faceafrica.com/article/nana-buluku-the-revered-goddess-and-supreme-deity-of-west-africa-and-the-caribbean

Kerestetzi, K. (2018). The spirit of a place: materiality, spatiality, and feeling in Afro-American religions. Journal de La Société Des Américanistes, 104(104–1). https://doi.org/10.4000/jsa.15573

Koutonin, M. (2020, February 3). Story of cities #5: Benin

References

City, the mighty medieval capital now lost without trace. The Guardian. https://www.theguardian.com/cities/2016/mar/18/story-of-cities-5-benin-city-edo-nigeria-mighty-medieval-capital-lost-without-trace

Kwekudee. (2013, December 11). Olokun Deity and its various Olokun festivals. Kwekudee Trip Down Memory Lane. https://kwekudee-tripdownmemorylane.blogspot.com/2013/12/olokun-deity-and-its-various-olokun.html

Landes, R., & Cole, S. (2006). The city of women (2nd ed.). University of New Mexico Press.

Lawal, B. (1985). Orí: The significance of the head in Yoruba sculpture. Journal of Anthropological Research, 41(1), 91–103. https://doi.org/10.1086/jar.41.1.3630272

Lele, Ó. (2000). The secrets of Afro-Cuban divination: How to cast the Diloggún, the Oracle of the Orishas (0 ed.). Destiny Books.

Magia-afro-latino. (2014, April 17). Afro-Latino Spirituality. https://magia-afro-latino.tumblr.com/post/82965516117/myoruba-nana-buruk%C3%BA-is-the-great-grandmother-to

Masquelier, A., Stewart, C., & Shaw, R. (1997). Syncretism/Anti-syncretism: The politics of religious synthesis. Journal of Religion in Africa, 27(2), 177. https://doi.org/10.2307/1581685

Myoruba. (2014, June 19). My Yoruba. https://myoruba.tumblr.com/post/89265416397/oyas-herbs

Nigeria. (2020, December 1). United States Department of State. https://www.state.gov/reports/2018-report-on-international-religious-freedom/nigeria/

Olayiwola, A. (2021, May 10). Nigerian eggplant stew. Eat Well Abi. https://eatwellabi.com/nigerian-eggplant-stew/

Olomola, I. (1988). Contradictions in Yoruba folk beliefs concerning post-life existence : the ado example. Journal Des Africanistes, 58(1), 107–118. https://doi.org/10.3406/jafr.1988.2255

References

Oshun, O. (2016, December 24). Omo-oshun. Yalorde. https://omo-oshun.tumblr.com/post/154882187128

Oshun, O. (2009). Oddun of Ita or Consulta for the diviner : Okana Sorde (1) "Where the world began with one", To Obara (6) "A King should not lie ".

Park, G. K. (n.d.). Divination. Encyclopedia Britannica. Retrieved May 11, 2021, from https://www.britannica.com/topic/divination

Prayers. (n.d.). Catholic Online. Retrieved May 12, 2021, from https://www.catholic.org/prayers/

SELKA, S. (2010). Morality in the religious marketplace: Evangelical Christianity, Candomblé, and the struggle for moral distinction in Brazil. American Ethnologist, 37(2), 291–307. https://doi.org/10.1111/j.1548-1425.2010.01256.x

Simpkins, P. C. (2016, June). The absent agronomist and the Lord of Poison: Cultivating modernity in transatlantic literature, 1758–1854. College of Social Sciences and Humanities of Northeastern University. https://repository.library.northeastern.edu/files

Slavery and remembrance. (n.d.-a). Slavery and Remembrance. Retrieved May 9, 2021, from http://slaveryandremembrance.org/articles/article/?id=A0060

Soyinka, W. (1990). Myth, literature and the African world (Reprint ed.). Cambridge University Press.

Staff, E. W. H. S. (2018, May 5). Yorubic medicine: The art of divine herbology. East West School of Planetary Herbology. https://planetherbs.com/research-center/theory-articles/yorubic-medicine-the-art-of-divine-herbology/

The Choices Program. (2017, September 22). Who was François Makandal? Choices Program. https://www.choices.edu/video/who-was-francois-makandal/

The Orishas: Nana Buruku. (2016, September 8). Original Botanica. https://www.originalbotanica.com/blog/orishas-nana-buruku-santeria/

Unitarian Universalist Association. (2020, August 4). The

References

Promise and the practice: Story for all ages. UUA.Org. https://www.uua.org/worship/words/time-all-ages/promise-and-practice-story-all-ages

Vanzant, I. (2020, December 14). 4 Core principles of Yoruba spirituality. Omega. https://www.eomega.org/videos/4-core-principles-of-yoruba-spirituality#

Vodou.Dialogue Institute. (2020, September 16). Dialogue InstituteVodou. https://dialogueinstitute.org/afrocaribbean-and-african-religion-information/2020/9/16/vodou

Wall, K., & Clerici, C. (2015, November 29). Vodou is elusive and endangered, but it remains the soul of Haitian people. The Guardian. https://www.theguardian.com/world/2015/nov/07/vodou-haiti-endangered-faith-soul-of-haitian-people

Wyndham, J. (1921). Myths of Ife. London.

Yoruba medicine, Roman Catholicism and the birth of Santeria. (2020, April 29). [Video]. YouTube. https://www.youtube.com/watch?v=NPCpBwUMFkE

About the Author

Monique Joiner Siedlak is a writer, witch, and warrior on a mission to awaken people to their greatest potential through the power of storytelling infused with mysticism, modern paganism, and new age spirituality. At the young age of 12, she began rigorously studying the fascinating philosophy of Wicca. By the time she was 20, she was self-initiated into the craft, and hasn't looked back ever since. To this day, she has authored over 40 books pertaining to the magick and mysteries of life.

To find out more about Monique Joiner Siedlak artistically, spiritually, and personally, feel free to visit her **official website**.

www.mojosiedlak.com

facebook.com/mojosiedlak
twitter.com/mojosiedlak
instagram.com/mojosiedlak
pinterest.com/mojosiedlak
bookbub.com/authors/monique-joiner-siedlak

More Books by Monique

African Spirituality Beliefs and Practices
Hoodoo
Seven African Powers: The Orishas
Cooking for the Orishas
Lucumi: The Ways of Santeria
Voodoo of Louisiana
Haitian Vodou
Orishas of Trinidad
Connecting With Your Ancestors
Black Magic
The Orishas
Vodun: West Africa's Spiritual Life

Practical Magick
Wiccan Basics
Candle Magick
Wiccan Spells
Love Spells
Abundance Spells
Herb Magick

More Books by Monique

Moon Magick
Creating Your Own Spells
Gypsy Magic
Protection Magick
Celtic Magick

Personal and Self Development

Creative Visualization
Astral Projection for Beginners
Meditation for Beginners
Reiki for Beginners
Manifesting With the Law of Attraction
Stress Management
Being an Empath Today

Get a Handle on Life

Get a Handle on Anxiety
Get a Handle on Depression
Get a Handle on Procrastination

The Yoga Collective

Yoga for Beginners
Yoga for Stress
Yoga for Back Pain
Yoga for Weight Loss
Yoga for Flexibility
Yoga for Advanced Beginners
Yoga for Fitness
Yoga for Runners
Yoga for Energy
Yoga for Your Sex Life
Yoga to Beat Depression and Anxiety
Yoga for Menstruation
Yoga to Detox Your Body

More Books by Monique

Yoga to Tone Your Body

A Natural Beautiful You
Creating Your Own Body Butter
Creating Your Own Body Scrub
Creating Your Own Body Spray

Last Chance Join My Newsletter!

If you missed it, I have a free gift available for you and wanted to remind you it's still available.

mojosiedlak.com/newsletter-signup

Thank you for reading my book.
I really appreciate all your feedback and would love to hear what you have to say! Please leave your review at your favorite retailer!

Thank you

www.ingramcontent.com/pod-product-compliance
Lightning Source LLC
Chambersburg PA
CBHW060834050426
42453CB00008B/694